Lecture Notes in Economics and Mathematical Systems

Managing Editors: M. Beckmann and W. Krelle

349

Gerard A. Pfann

Dynamic Modelling of Stochastic Demand for Manufacturing Employment

Springer-Verlag

Berlin Heidelberg New York London
Paris Tokyo Hong Kong Barcelona

Managing Editors
Prof. Dr. M. Beckmann
Brown University
Providence, RI 02912, USA

Prof. Dr. W. Krelle
Institut für Gesellschafts- und Wirtschaftswissenschaften
der Universität Bonn
Adenauerallee 24−42, D-5300 Bonn, FRG

Author
Dr. Gerard A. Pfann
University of Limburg, Department of Economics
P.O. Box 616, 6200 MD Maastricht, The Netherlands

ISBN 3-540-52881-4 Springer-Verlag Berlin Heidelberg New York
ISBN 0-387-52881-4 Springer-Verlag New York Berlin Heidelberg

Printing and binding: Druckhaus Beltz, Hemsbach/Bergstr.
2142/3140-543210 − Printed on acid-free paper

In memory of Frederik G.H. Furnée.

CONTENTS

CHAPTER 1 : INTRODUCTION

The objective of this dissertation is to provide new theoretical as well as empirical insights into the decisive elements of firms' labour demand through time, by generalizing existing labour demand models derived from theories about decision making under uncertainty. The models will be applied to time series data of the manufacturing sector in the Netherlands and U.K. for blue and white collar employment, using recently developed econometric techniques, in order to examine the empirical applicability of the models.

Labour is a quasi-fixed production factor, that is, a production factor whose total employments costs are partially variable and partially fixed. The first economist to successfully uphold this thesis was Walter Oi in 1962 (cf. Oi, 1962). From an employer's point of view, the dynamics of labour demand are largely due to hiring and firing costs that exist next to regular payroll costs, when the firm changes its productive workforce. Consequently, future expectations have become an important issue in modelling employment decisions in a dynamic context.

In 1976 Lucas criticised the way in which econometricians modelled the reactions of economic agents to exogenous shocks in their environment. Lucas's critique was focussed on the behavioural invariance of econometric models in the presence of changes in the nature of these shocks. Proper models, he argued, must embody an implicit rule of adaptation to stochastic shocks, or "stochastically disturbed functions of the state of the system" (Lucas, 1976, p.40).

Oi's views on quasi-fixedness of labour and the Lucas-critique were integrated in Sargent's (1978) model for dynamic labour demand schedules. Sargent asserts that entrepreneurs determine labour demand at time t jointly with a contingency plan for future labour input, maximizing their firm's expected real present value of profits. At time t+1 current employment decisions and future input schemes are revised in the light of new information that has become available. The occurence of hiring and/or firing costs, generally referred to as adjustment costs of labour (ACL), prevent firms from instantaneously adjusting the productive workforce to changes in the economic environment. Generalizations of Sargent's (1978) model play a central role in this dissertation.

Nickell (1986) presented an overview of what was known up until the early eighties about the size and structure of ACL, and surveyed dynamic models of labour demand. In addition to Nickell's survey table I.1 presents an overview of the main econometric studies which examine interrelated input decisions of production factors. Although already in 1974 Nadiri and Rosen pointed out

Table I.1 : Survey of Interrelated Factor Demand Models.

AGGREGATE LABOUR, CAPITAL (+ MATERIALS, ENERGY)

					Variable Inputs	Quasi-fixed Inputs	Expectations
Nadiri & Rosen	1969	Q: 1947.I-62.IV	US	Ma		Blue collar workers, Hours worked, Capital, Utilization Rate	Static
Berndt, Fuss, Waverman	1979	A: 1947-74	US	Ma	Labour, Energy, Materials	Capital	Static
Meese	1980	Q: 1947.I-62.IV	US	Ma		Labour, Capital	Rational
Hansen & Sargent	1981	Theoretical				Labour, Capital	Rational
McIntosh	1982	A: 1950-73	UK	Ag		Labour, Capital	Static
Pindyck & Rotemberg	1983a	A: 1948-71	US	Ma	Energy, Materials	Labour, Capital	Rational
Epstein & Denny	1983	A: 1947-76	US	Ma	Materials	Labour, Capital	Static
Eichenbaum	1984	M: 1959.I-78.12	US	Ma		Hours Worked, Inventories	Rational
Epstein & Yatchew	1985	A: 1947-76	US	Ma		Labour, Capital	Nonstatic
Harris	1985	Q: 1968.I-81.IV	UK	E		Hours worked, Capital, Utilization rate	Nonstatic
Kokkelenberg & Bisschoff	1986	Q: 1959.III-77.IV	US	Ma	Labour, Energy	Capital	Weakly rational
Holly & Smith	1986	Q: 1968.III-79.III	UK	Ma		Labour, Capital	Static
Kollintzas & Cassings	1986	Theoretical	US	Ma	Energy, Materials	Labour, Capital	Rational
Morrison	1986	A: 1947-81	US	Ma	Labour, Energy, Materials	Capital	Nonstatic

TWO TYPES OF LABOUR AND CAPITAL

					Variable Inputs	Quasi-fixed Inputs	Expectations
Nadiri & Rosen	1974	Q: 1947.I-67.IV	US	Ma		Blue collar workers, White collar workers, hours worked, Capital, Utilization rate, Inventories	Static
Pindyck & Rotemberg	1983b	A: 1947-76	US	Ma	Blue collar workers	White collar workers, Capital	Rational
Kokkelenberg	1984	Q: 1947.I-79.IV	US	Ma	Blue collar workers, Inventories, Hours worked	White collar workers, Capital	Nonstatic
Shapiro	1986	Q:1955.I-80.IV	US	Ma		Blue collar workers, White collar workers, Hours worked, Capital	Rational

A = annual; Q = quarterly; M = monthly; E = engineering; Ma = manufacturing; Ag = aggregate

that employment decisions for production workers differ from those of nonproduction workers, due to differences in hiring costs and firing costs, only few authors have considered more than one (aggregate) type of labour in their models.

As the overview in table I.1 also shows, existing dynamic labour demand models mainly differ in the way expectations are modelled. In models with <u>static</u> expectations, variables that are beyond the direct influence of the firm are assumed to be stationary. At some initial time t the firm chooses the optimal time path for the decision variables by maximizing an intertemporal objective function. The plan remains unchanged through time, regardless of the new information that becomes available and unexpected changes that may take place. The driving forces of the economy are considered to be beyond the scope of this kind of model. Empirical applications are usually based on detrended stationary data.

In <u>nonstatic</u> expectations models, it is assumed that "decisions made by optimizing the objective function with stochastic variables replaced by their conditional expectations are close enough approximations to those which would result if the expected values were maximized" (Morrison, 1986, p.366). Future expectations of exogenous variables are obtained from solutions of ARIMA equations. The nonstationarity of the series of production factors is assumed to be deterministic, and is remedied by incorporating deterministic trends.

In _rational_ expectations labour demand models economic agents (e.g. representative firms) use current available and relevant information (and, consequently, do not use past information only) in order to maximize the expected real present value of profits over a future time horizon. The stochastic process of exogenous variables is used in forming expectations. In each period, expectations and contingency plans are revised in the light of new information. As a result, rational expectations models should not be subject to the Lucas critique.

If an econometric model has been derived from economic theory, its parameters have an economic interpretation. It is possible that the parameters of the stochastic processes of exogenous forcing variables partially define the parameters of the econometric model for the endogenous variables. For example, assume that wages are weakly exogenous with respect to employment. This means that past realizations of employment have no effect on current realizations of wage rates. Assume also that past realizations of wage rates however do play a role in the explanation of current employment levels. This is called unidirectional Granger-causality from wages to employment, which happens in a perfectly competitive labour market where firms are assumed to be price-takers. Now, let a structural break occur in the process that generates wages, consequently changing (some of) the parameters of the wage equation. Under rational expectations this structural break will have an impact on the parameters of the employment equation.

The underlying economic theory often imposes overidentifying restrictions on parameters of the econometric model for the endogenous variables. Structural parameters can be estimated and their plausibility can be examined provided they are identified. Useful insights into parameter identification can be obtained from closed form solutions of the firm's maximization problem first order (Euler) conditions (cf. Hansen and Sargent, 1980, 1981)). Closed form solutions of multivariate linear rational expectations models were provided by Kollintzas (1985). He showed that the forward looking solution of these models are uniquely determined in terms of structural parameters.

Dynamic factor demand rational expectations models often fail to pass tests on overidentifying restrictions. It has been argued that the reason for this failure may possibly be the simple quadratic specification of structural models from which linear reduced form demand equations are derived. Attempts to overcome this criticism have principally lead to generalizations of production, profit or cost functions (e.g. Berndt and Morrison

(1981), Pindyck and Rotemberg (1983a,b)). However, since the dynamics of labour demand in these models are mainly the result of adjustment costs, one should seriously question the appropriateness of the quadratic shape of adjustment cost functions introduced by Holt, Modigliani, Muth and Simon in 1960 (cf. Holt et.al. (1960)) and used in many studies since then.

Recently, some evidence has been given for ACL functions not being stable through time. Smith (1984) has found the speed of workforce adjustment to be positively related to the rate of unemployment. Burgess (1988) has found evidence for a significant effect on ACL of labour market legislations, labour market tightness, and union power. Hamermesh (1988) shows that non-convexities of the ACL function (fixed costs) give rise to lumpy adjustment of the firm's workforce to its target level. These authors model the costs that depend on the extent of labour adjustment through a quadratic ACL specification.

In this dissertation, existing rational expectations adjustment costs models for labour demand will be reconsidered, refined, generalized and applied to employment data in manufacturing in the Netherlands and in the UK. Stochastic optimal control techniques and recent econometric methods are used in the analysis. Each chapter has been written such, that it can be read separately from the others. The dissertation is organized as follows.

In chapter 2 a prototype model of dynamic labour demand is presented. We modify Sargent's (1978) model and apply it to the
demand of blue and white collar workers in the Dutch manufacturing sector. The empirical application is carried out using
stochastic stationary variables. Nonstationarity in the time
series have been removed through detrending of the data prior to
estimation of the model. The two types of labour are assumed to
have different wage costs, different productivity and different
adjustment costs. We show that Sargent unnecessarily restricts
the model in order to estimate the structural parameters.
Moreover, it is shown that the structural parameters of the
model are identified.

In chapter 3, the bivariate labour demand model is extended as
follows. Blue and white collar labour demand are assumed to be
interrelated. This means that lagged values of wage costs and
employment of blue and white collar labour play an important
role in the determination of current levels of white collar
workers. Employment decisions are assumed to be taken conditionally on the capital stock. In contrast to the existing
literature and in extension of chapter 2, where the nonstationarity of the series of production factor inputs is viewed to
be nuisance that is beyond the scope of the theoretical model,
we model the nonstationarity of labour demand as being induced

by the nonstationarity of real wage costs and capital. Following Blanchard and Kahn (1980), we use a methodology that differs from Kollintzas (1985), which allows us to express the closed form solutions of more general linear interrelated labour demand models in terms of structural parameters.

The solution of the stochastic quadratic control problem, applied in chapter 3 for the examination of a bivariate labour demand model with capital being predetermined, is used in chapter 4 to get more insights into the restrictions on the parameters of multivariate flexible accelerator models (see e.g. Treadway (1971), Epstein and Denny (1983)), in which labour and capital are determined simultaneously. Compared with Epstein and Yatchew (1985), we obtain optimal production factor trajectories without previously specifying an expectations formation process.

In line with the Lucas critique, we analyse the impact of structural changes in the processes of exogenous variables on demand for aggregate labour and capital in the Dutch manufacturing sector. We examine how the impacts of oil shocks, occurring in 1973.IV and 1979.II, on real input prices influenced factor demand.

The identified structural parameters of the models presented in

the chapters 2, 3 and 4 are estimated using a two step estimation procedure proposed by Chamberlain (1982) and Gouriéroux
et.al. (1985). In a first stage, an unrestricted version of the
reduced form of the model is estimated that incorporates the
restrictions on the order of the system implied by the
underlying theory. The identified structural parameters are
often nonlinearly related to the parameters estimated in the
first stage. In the second stage, the structural parameters are
estimated using the method of Asymptotic Least Squares (ALS)
which minimizes the distance between the unrestricted reduced
form estimates and the reduced form coefficients expressed as
functions of the basic structural parameters. The ALS procedure
is asymptotically equivalent to Maximum Likelihood (ML) estimation methods, provided ML estimates of the parameter estimates
from the first stage are used together with an optimal weighting
matrix and all restrictions between structural parameters and
reduced form coefficients have been imposed. In order to obtain
the weighting matrix the derivatives of the nonlinear relationships between the parameters estimated in the first stage
and the structural parameters are needed (see also Appendix
A.1).

Chapter 5 examines the appropriateness of the hypothesis of
quadratic adjustment costs with respect to dynamic labour

demand. Quadratic ACL functions are symmetric. That is, the costs a firm faces when an amount of new workers are hired (such as expenditures on advertising, screening and training) vary in the same way as when the same number of workers are fired. The quadratic assumption is made mainly for analytical convenience and computational ease, and is most probably at variance with the real structural form of ACL, since "there is no reason for hiring costs to be symmetric" (Nickell, 1986, p.478).

To get information on the shape of the adjustment costs, we interviewed personnel managers of Dutch manufacturing firms. The interviews focussed on decisions of firms to change their productive workforce, and the costs that arise from these changes. Based on the outcome of the interviews, we propose a new ACL specification. The merit of the specification is the possibility to measure the difference between hiring costs and firing costs of labour, whereby the asymmetry parameter in the specification can be interpreted as a relative measure of the adjustment speed of labout to a target level of employment which increases in periods of economic uprise and decreases in recessions.

Chapter 6 overcomes one of the shortcomings of the linear rational expectations labour demand model. We use the more general asymmetric functional form as put forward and tested in

chapter 5 to model adjustment costs. We present a multivariate
asymmetric adjustment costs model of the firm's labour demand,
in which the symmetric linear rational expectations model in
nested. We analyse two intertemporal models for employment
decisions. One model takes capital as a predetermined factor
with respect to employment decisions. The second assumes capital and employment to be simultaneously determined. Further, we
examine the impacts of unanticipated shocks in real wage costs,
labour productivity or technology on factor input decisions. We
report empirical evidence for the two models, using Dutch and
U.K. manufacturing time series. We separately examine the
firm's demand for blue and white collar labour allowing for differences in adjustment costs for the two types of labour. In
this way we try to circumvent misleading (with regard to adjustment costs) explanations of employment dynamics in terms of
aggregation (cf. Nickell (1984)). We apply the generalized
method of moments (GMM) technique of Hansen (1982) in order to
estimate the structural parameters of the nonlinear first order
conditions derived from the intertemporal optimization model.
Among the authors who estimate first order conditions of factor
demand models we mention Kennan (1979), Pindyck and Rotemberg
(1983a,b) and Shapiro (1986).

Finally, in chapter 7 the general findings presented in this dissertation are evaluated, and a summary and conclusions are given.

CHAPTER 2 : A PROTOTYPE MODEL FOR BLUE AND WHITE COLLAR EMPLOYMENT DECISIONS OF RATIONAL ENTREPRENEURS UNDER UNCERTAINTY

2.1 Introduction

In this chapter we present a prototype model for labour demand in the Dutch manufacturing sector assuming that firms face adjustment costs and operate under uncertainty. Labour demand consists of blue and white collar workers. We use quarterly data for the period 1971.I – 1984.IV to estimate the model. We modify Sargent's (1978) paper on dynamic labour demand schedules. Using a closed form solution of a linear rational expectation model in which adjustment costs play a dominant role, we show that the structural parameters of the underlying economic theory are identified.

Chapter 2 is organized as follows. In section 2 empirical evidence is presented for unidirectional causality (in the sense of Granger) of wage costs to employment. Section 3 models the demand for blue and white collar labour and derives a closed form solution in terms of underlying structural parameters for a bivariate linear symmetric rational expectations model without

13

interrelatedness of lagged employment decisions of the two types of labour.

In section 4 the structural parameters are efficiently estimated using ALS.
ALS is also used to estimate standard errors for the parameters of production and cost functions. At this point we notice that Sargent does not give standard errors for the estimated parameters of interest.

The overidentifying restrictions implied by the underlying theoretical model are tested using a likelihood ratio type test. The appropriateness of the model is checked by means of a multivariate portmanteau test on residual autocorrelation. Finally, the moving average representation of the model is reported along with percentage forecast error variance decompositions implied by vector autoregressions. The results suggest comple mentarity over time between the two types of labour, a strong correlation between their wage costs, due to the way in which increases in wages and salaries are stipulated in labour contracts, and empirical support of Oi's (1962) hypothesis about the quasi-fixedness of costly adjustable labour. Section 5 concludes this chapter.

2.2 Wage costs, Employment and Causality

Wage costs and demand for labour are related over time. For instance Nefçti (1978) and Sargent (1978) find empirical evidence for unidirectional Granger causality of wages to employment for post-World War II U.S. manufacturing data. Before investigating the dynamics between wages and employment the appropriate time series have to be selected. As the figures in table II.1 indicate, there exists a considerable difference between hourly wages and wage costs per worker in the Netherlands in the period 1971-1984. This discrepancy is due to holiday allowances and social premiums paid by the employer. Assuming that the employment decisions of firms result from a cost-benefit analysis, it is appropriate to choose the wage costs series instead of the wage itself.

Table II.1 : Gross hourly wage and wage costs in the Dutch manufacturing sector in Dutch Guilders (current prices)

	1971	1972	1973	1974	1975	1976	1977
Gross hourly wage	6.53	7.23	8.26	9.62	10.97	12.19	13.28
Wage costs per hour	11.76	13.10	14.78	17.06	19.00	20.90	22.70
Difference in %	80.1	81.2	78.9	77.3	73.2	71.6	70.8

	1978	1979	1980	1981	1982	1983	1984
Gross hourly wage	14.23	15.04	15.85	16.96	18.37	19.08	19.54
Wage costs per hour	25.23	27.05	28.40	29.90	32.03	33.61	35.18
Difference in %	77.3	79.9	79.2	76.3	74.4	76.2	80.0

Source : Central Bureau of Statistics.

The data we used to study the causal relation between real wage costs and employment of blue and white collar workers in the Dutch manufacturing sector are quarterly data for the period 1971.I - 1984.IV. A description of the data and their sources is given in appendix V. We ignore the possible influence of other time series. That is, the information set used to test the causality hypothesis omits information about time series, other than wage costs and employment. To check the direction of causality, we have chosen reasonably long autoregressions. High order autoregressions should provide a rather good approximation for the second moments of a stationary stochastic process, thereby avoiding that possible omission of past values with large coefficients induces spurious significant coefficients on lagged values of other exogenous variables (Geweke, 1978). Consequently for the aim of testing causality a simple (linear) model with long lags will probably be sufficient. The length of the lagged endogenous variable is fixed at two years and the possible Granger-causing variable is lagged one year. More explicitly, the following bivariate model is considered.

$$W_t = \text{deterministic part} + \sum_{k=1}^{8} \omega_{1k} W_{t-k} + \sum_{l=1}^{4} \eta_{11} N_{t-1} + \epsilon_{1t}$$

$$N_t = \text{deterministic part} + \sum_{k=1}^{4} \omega_{2k} W_{t-k} + \sum_{l=1}^{8} \eta_{21} N_{t-1} + \epsilon_{2t}$$

where W = real wage costs, N = number of people employed. The deterministic part consists of a constant, trend, quadratic trend and 3 seasonal dummies, and $(\epsilon_{1t}, \epsilon_{2t})' \sim IIN(0, \Sigma_2)$.

If the real wage costs are Granger-caused by employment we should reject the hypothesis $H_1 : \eta_{1l} = 0$, $l = 1, \ldots 4$ as being invalid. Analogously the hypothesis $H_2 : \omega_{2k} = 0$, $k = 1, \ldots 4$ should be rejected when wages Granger-cause the employment level. The bivariate model is estimated for blue collar workers as well as for white collar workers. Testing for H_1 we find likelihood ratio (LR) test statistics of 1.98 and 1.30 for blue and white collar workers respectively. The hypothesis H_1 cannot be rejected at the conventional significance level of 5% for either sort of labour. The LR-statistics for H_2 equal 11.64 and 9.40 respectively. These results indicate unidirectional causality from the real wage costs to employment in both cases.

Alternatively, we can take into account mutual influences between the two labour categories. Consequently we have fitted the data to a four-variate vector AR(4) model for wage costs and employment, with deterministic part being identical to that of the previous model. Then it is possible to test simultaneously for feasible causal relations between the two wage costs series on the one hand and the employment series on the other. A Wald test based on OLS estimates of the unrestricted four variate model can straightforwardly be carried out. The hypothesis H_1 and H_2 are defined in accordance with the definitions above, aside from the fact that either hypothesis now implies eight restrictions (instead of four in the previous model). We find a Wald test statistic for the restrictions that employment does not Granger-cause wage costs of blue and white collar workers of 7.80.

The Wald test statistic of the hypothesis that wage costs do not Granger-cause employment equals 31.44.

In conclusions we can say that these results are similar to the Neftçi-Sargent finding on causality : Unidirectional causality from the real wage costs to employment is in accordance with the information in the data for both categories of labour in the Dutch industrial sector.

2.3 Modelling the Demand for Labour

In this section, we introduce the theoretical model and we derive the implications of the theory for the time series process of wage costs and employment. We assume that a representative firm hires blue and white collar workers denoted by n_1 and n_2 respectively. The short-run production function (PF) of the firm is specified as

$$\text{(II.1)} \quad Y_t(n_{1t}, n_{2t}) = \sum_{i=1}^{2} \{(\alpha_{i1} + s_{it})n_{it} - \tfrac{1}{2}\alpha_{i2}n_{it}^2\}; \quad \alpha_{i1} > 0,$$

$$\alpha_{i2} > 0, \quad i = 1,2, \quad t = 0,1,2,\ldots.$$

The rate of output per period of time is denoted by Y_t, α_{i1} and α_{i2} are constant parameters. Because capital is assumed not to be a decision variable in the short-run, it is assumed to be predetermined, and not explicitly included in the production function. The variables s_{1t} and s_{2t} are exogenous stochastic shocks of the production. The production function is specified in such a way that conditional on n_{it}, average productivity follows a stationary stochastic process s_{it}. At every point in time a firm maximizes the expected real present value of profits given all the available information. In reaction to a change in the environment such as for instance a change in relative factor prices or a shock in product demand, the firm will follow the same decision rule. But the result of the decision will depend on the realization of the exogenous shocks. A quadratic PF locally approximates the range of diminishing productivity of factors of production.

In line with the literature on dynamic factor demand models (e.g. Holt, et al. (1960); Nickell (1986)), we assume that the adjustment cost function is quadratic. The adjustment costs of a reduction of the number of people employed, which are firing

costs and the loss of firm specific knowledge are very difficult
to measure.   Although it is very unlikely that the costs of a
reduction of the workforce will be similar to the costs of
expansion, for computational ease, we assume a symmetric adjustment cost function

$$(II.2) \quad AC_t(n_{1t},n_{2t}) = \sum_{i=1}^{2} \tfrac{1}{2}\beta_i(\Delta n_{it})^2 \; ; \; \beta_i > 0, \; i=1,2.$$

The real adjustment costs β_i are assumed to be constant.
Normally, white collar workers will be employed in positions for
which more job-specific knowledge is required.   The hiring procedure will be more expensive, and the time before they are productive will be longer.   Therefore, it seems quite plausible
that the adjustment costs for white collar workers will be
higher than those for blue collar workers, i.e. $\beta_2 > \beta_1$.
The variable wage costs are assumed to be proportional to the
number of workers employed :

$$(II.3) \quad W_t(n_{1t},n_{2t}) = \sum_{i=1}^{2} w_{it} \, n_{it}.$$

The firm uses the relevant information up to time t, including
the real wage costs per worker at time t, denoted by w_{1t} and w_{2t}
respectively, to choose contingency plans for the employment of
blue and white collar workers.   In order to determine the actual

20

optimal employment decisions at time t, the rational entrepreneur has to plan future employment decisions. He will revise his plans at time t+1 in the light of new information. The firm's objective is to maximize its real present value at time t, that is

$$(II.4) \quad \text{Max } PV_t = \text{Max } E_t \sum_{j=0}^{\infty} \tau^j [Y_{t+j} - AC_{t+j} - W_{t+j}]; \quad 0 < \tau < 1.$$

The operator E_t is defined as the conditional expectations $E_t \ x \equiv E(x|\Omega_t)$, where x is a random variable and Ω_t is the set of information available to the firm at time t, which includes s_t and w_t; τ is a real discount factor. For the sake of simplicity of the notation, the arguments of the functions in (II.4) have been deleted. First order necessary conditions for maximization of (II.4) consist of the Euler equations and a pair of transversality conditions which assure the finiteness of the process (see e.g. Sargent, 1979, chpts. 9 and 14).

The solution at time t of the Euler equations to this infinite time horizon problem, which satisfy the transversality conditions is as follows

$$(II.5) \quad E_t \ n_{it+1} = k_i \ n_{it} - \tau^{-1} n_{it-1} - (\beta_i \tau)^{-1} (\alpha_{1i} - w_{it} + s_{it}),$$

$$\text{with } k_i = (\beta_i(\tau+1) + \alpha_{2i})/\beta_i \tau, \quad i=1.2.$$

According to (II.5), at time t, the expected or planned employment level in period t+1 is linearly related to the current and one period lagged employment level and to the current wage costs.

The expected or planned value of n_i in the future, $E_t\, n_{it+1}$, can not be observed as such but has to be determined in the model. To find a solution of the Euler linear difference model under rational expectations, we follow Blanchard & Kahn (1980) and augment (II.5) as follows

$$(II.6) \quad \begin{bmatrix} n_{1t} \\ n_{2t} \\ E_t n_{1t+1} \\ E_t n_{2t+1} \end{bmatrix} = \begin{bmatrix} 0 & I_2 \\ & \\ A_1 & A_2 \end{bmatrix} \begin{bmatrix} n_{1t-1} \\ n_{2t-1} \\ n_{1t} \\ n_{2t} \end{bmatrix} + \begin{bmatrix} 0 \\ \\ \Gamma_0 \end{bmatrix} z_t$$

with A_1 being a 2 × 2 diagonal matrix with $-\tau^{-1}$ on the diagonal,

$$A_2 = \begin{bmatrix} k_1 & 0 \\ 0 & k_2 \end{bmatrix} \qquad \Gamma_0 = \begin{bmatrix} -\alpha_{11}/\beta_1\tau & 1/\beta_1\tau & 0 \\ -\alpha_{12}/\beta_2\tau & 0 & 1/\beta_2\tau \end{bmatrix}, \text{ and }$$

$z_{it}' = (1 \ w_{1t} - s_{1t} \ w_{2t} - s_{2t})'$; $i=1,\ldots,4$; $z_t = (z_{1t},\ldots,z_{4t})'$.

We transform the companion matrix $A = \begin{bmatrix} 0 & I_2 \\ A_1 & A_2 \end{bmatrix}$ into Jordan's canonical form $A = C^{-1} \Lambda C$, where C^{-1} consists of eigenvectors of A associated with the eigenvalues on the diagonal of matrix Λ.

Λ is partitioned as $\Lambda = \begin{bmatrix} \Lambda_1 & 0 \\ 0 & \Lambda_2 \end{bmatrix}$, where Λ_1 has on the diagonal

all the eigenvalues of A, that lie on or within the unit circle

and Λ_2 contains all the eigenvalues that lie outside the unit

circle. The number of diagonal elements of Λ_2 defines the

number of stationarity solutions of the difference equations in

(II.6). For models with a quadratic objective function the

number of eigenvalues greater than one equals the number of

eigenvalues within the unit circle (see e.g. Kollintzas, 1985).

This implies that both Λ_1 and Λ_2 are diagonal matrices of order

2, and that a unique, stationary forward looking solution exists

for the expectations variables.

Partitioning C in accordance with Λ the unique solution of the

Euler equations (see Blanchard & Kahn (1980)) at time t can be

expressed as

$$n_t = -C_{22}^{-1} C_{21} n_{t-1} - C_{22}^{-1} \sum_{i=0}^{\infty} \Lambda_2^{-i-1} C_{22} \Gamma_0 E_t(z_{t+i}|\Omega_t),$$

where $n_t = (n_{1t}, n_{2t})'$. As C_{22}^{-1} and Λ_2 are diagonal and $-C_{22}^{-1}C_{21} = \Lambda_1$, the solution can be simplified further to become

$$(II.7) \quad n_t = \Lambda_1 n_{t-1} - \sum_{i=0}^{\infty} \Lambda_2^{-i-1} \Gamma_0 E_t(z_{t+i}|\Omega_t).$$

In (II.7) the employment level in period t is expressed as a

linear relationship of the employment level in the previous

period and of the expected values of the exogenous variables z over the infinite future horizon. The parameters in (II.7) are nonlinear functions of the structural parameters in the objective function (II.4). More specifically, the eigenvalues of A which are the diagonal elements of Λ, can be expressed as follows

$$\lambda_1 = \tfrac{1}{2} k_2 + \tfrac{1}{2} \sqrt{k_2^2 - 4/\tau} \quad , \quad \lambda_2 = \tfrac{1}{2} k_2 - \tfrac{1}{2} \sqrt{k_2^2 - 4/\tau} \quad ,$$

$$\lambda_3 = \tfrac{1}{2} k_1 + \tfrac{1}{2} \sqrt{k_1^2 - 4/\tau} \quad , \quad \lambda_4 = \tfrac{1}{2} k_1 - \tfrac{1}{2} \sqrt{k_1^2 - 4/\tau} \quad .$$

From the assumption that the parameters α_{21}, α_{22}, β_1, β_2 and the real discount factor τ are nonnegative, it follows that

$$| \lambda_1 | > 1; \quad | \lambda_2 | \leq 1; \quad | \lambda_3 | > 1; \quad | \lambda_4 | \leq 1.$$

The matrix C^{-1} partitioned according to Λ can be written as

$$C^{-1} = \begin{bmatrix} 1 & 0 & 1 & 0 \\ 0 & 1 & 0 & 1 \\ \lambda_4 & 0 & \lambda_3 & 0 \\ 0 & \lambda_2 & 0 & \lambda_1 \end{bmatrix} ; \quad \Lambda = \begin{bmatrix} \lambda_4 & 0 & 0 & 0 \\ 0 & \lambda_2 & 0 & 0 \\ 0 & 0 & \lambda_3 & 0 \\ 0 & 0 & 0 & \lambda_1 \end{bmatrix} .$$

By assuming linear stochastic processes for $s_t = (s_{1t}, s_{2t})'$ and $w_t = (w_{1t}, w_{2t})'$ we can express n_t in (II.7) as a linear function of observed variables, with parameters which are nonlinear functions of the structural parameters of production and labour costs functions and the parameters of the exogenous stochastic processes. Assuming that the stochastic components of labour productivity s_t are generated by a first order Markov process,

$$s_t = R \ s_{t-1} + \xi_t^s$$

where

$$R = \begin{bmatrix} \rho_1 & 0 \\ 0 & \rho_2 \end{bmatrix}; \ \xi_t^s = \begin{bmatrix} \xi_{1t} \\ \xi_{2t} \end{bmatrix}, \ \text{being an innovation with } E\xi_t^s = 0,$$

$E\xi_t^s \ \xi_t^{s'} = \Sigma_1$, we have

$$(II.8) \quad E_t \ s_{t+i} = R^i \ s_t, \ i \geq 0.$$

Further we assume that w_t is generated by a second order autoregressive process

$$(II.9) \quad w_t = C_0 + M_1 w_{t-1} + M_2 w_{t-2} + \xi_t^w$$

with constant term C_0, $M_j = \begin{bmatrix} \mu_{1j} & 0 \\ 0 & \mu_{2j} \end{bmatrix}$ and $\xi_t^w = \begin{bmatrix} \xi_{3t} \\ \xi_{4t} \end{bmatrix}$ being

the wage innovation with $E\xi_t^w = 0$ and $E \ \xi_t^w \ \xi_t^{w'} = \Sigma_2$.

We are looking for an explicit solution of the second right handside (r.h.s.) term of (II.7)

$$(II.10) \quad - \sum_{i=0}^{\infty} \Lambda_2^{-i-1} \Gamma_0 \ E_t \ (z_{t+i}) = \delta_0 + \sum_{i=0}^{\infty} \Lambda_2^{-i-1} \Gamma \ E_t \ (s_{t+i})$$

$$- \sum_{i=0}^{\infty} \Lambda_2^{-i-1} \Gamma \ E_t \ (w_{t+i}),$$

where δ_0 is a (2×1) vector with constant elements and

$$\Gamma = \begin{bmatrix} 1/\beta_1\tau & 0 \\ 0 & 1/\beta_2\tau \end{bmatrix}.$$

Substituting (II.8) into the second r.h.s. term of (II.10) and using the fact that Γ is diagonal, we find that

$$(II.11) \quad \sum_{i=0}^{\infty} \Lambda_2^{-i-1} \, \Gamma \, E_t \, (s_{t+i}) = P_1 s_t$$

where $P_1 = \Gamma \, \Lambda_2^{-1} \, (I - \Lambda_2^{-1} \, R)^{-1}$.

Similarly the third r.h.s. term of (II.10) can be expressed as

$$(II.12) \quad \Gamma \sum_{i=0}^{\infty} \Lambda_2^{-i-1} \, E_t \, (w_{t+i}) = P_2 \, (w_t + \Lambda_2^{-1} \, M_2 \, w_{t-1}),$$

where $P_2 = (I - \Lambda_2^{-1} \, M_1 - \Lambda_2^{-2} \, M_2)^{-1} \, \Gamma \, \Lambda_2^{-1}$,

as $E_t(w_{t+i}) = M_1 \, E_t(w_{t+i-1}) + M_2 \, E_t \, (w_{t+i-2})$ if we ignore the constant term. Substituting the expressions (II.10), (II.11) and (II.12) into (II.7), and deleting the constant terms [1], we find that

$$(II.13) \quad n_t = \Lambda_1 \, n_{t-1} + P_1 \, s_t - P_2 \, (w_t + \Lambda_2 \, M_2^{-1} w_{t-1}).$$

---

[1] The data used to estimate the parameters of the model have been adjusted for a constant, trend and seasonal dummies for reasons to be explained in section 4.

26

To eliminate the autocorrelation of s_t, we apply the Koyck transformation to (II.13). Unexpected economic changes will affect productivity (ξ_t^s) as well as wage costs (ξ_t^w). This effect is partly specific to productivity or wage costs, and it partly causes a mutually dependent innovation. Consequently, we substitute the process (II.9) for w_t to derive the reduced form of the joint process for w_t and n_t, which is a four variate autoregression of the form

(II.14a) $w_t = M_1\, w_{t-1} + M_2\, w_{t-2} + \xi_t^w$

(II.14b) $n_t = (R + \Lambda_1)n_{t-1} - R\,\Lambda_1\, n_{t-2} + P_2(R - M_1 - \Lambda^{-1}_2 M_2)w_{t-1}$

$\qquad\qquad P_2\, M_2\, (R\,\Lambda^{-1}_2 - I)\, w_{t-2} + P_1\, \xi_t^s - P_2\, \xi_t^w.$

The disturbance term $[\xi_t^w,\ (P_1\, \xi_t^s - P_2\, \xi_t^w)]'$ is assumed to be serially uncorrelated, normally distributed with mean zero and covariance matrix Σ, which is unrestricted (symmetric), as a result of the assumed diffusion of innovations in the system. The restricted model, expressed in structural parameters, follows from (II.14)

(II.15a) $w_{1t} = \mu_{11}\, w_{1t-1} + \mu_{12}\, w_{1t-2} + \xi_{1t}^w$

(II.15b) $w_{2t} = \mu_{21}\, w_{2t-1} + \mu_{22}\, w_{2t-2} + \xi_{2t}^w$

(II.15c) $n_{1t} = (\lambda_4 + \rho_1)n_{1t-1} - \lambda_4\rho_1 \, n_{1t-2} +$

$$\delta_1^{-1}(\rho_1 - \mu_{11} - \tau\lambda_4 \, \mu_{12})w_{1t-1} + \delta_1^{-1}(\mu_{12} \, (\tau\lambda_4\rho_1^{-1}))w_{1t-2}$$

$$+ \, e_{1t}$$

(II.15d) $n_{2t} = (\lambda_2 + \rho_2) \, n_{2t-1} - \lambda_2\rho_2 \, n_{2t-2} +$

$$\delta_2^{-1}(\rho_2 - \mu_{21} - \tau\lambda_2 \, \mu_{22})w_{2t-1} + \delta_2^{-1}(\mu_{22}(\tau\rho_2\lambda_2-1))w_{2t-2}$$

$$+ \, e_{2t}$$

where

$$\delta_1 = \tau\beta_1 \, (\lambda_3 - \mu_{11} - \mu_{12} \, \lambda_3^{-1}), \quad \delta_2 = \tau\beta_2 \, (\lambda_1 - \mu_{21} - \mu_{22} \, \lambda_1^{-1}),$$

and $(e_{1t} \, e_{2t})' = P_1 \, \xi_t^s - P_2 \, \xi_t^w$.

2.4 Empirical Results

In this section the model is estimated using quarterly data on employment (measured in thousands of men), and indices of real weekly wage costs of blue and white collar workers in the Dutch industrial sector.   These data are obtained from the Central Bureau of Statistics and cover the period from 1971.I through 1984.IV.   A more detailed description of the data is given in appendix V.   We assume that the impact of production factors, such as capital stock, which are not explicitly modelled, can be approximated by a deterministic trend.   Therefore, in a first instance, we detrend the data by regression using a constant, a linear and a quadratic trend and three seasonal dummies. The residuals from these regressions are used as data in the subsequent analysis.

An interesting feature of the causality hypothesis is that it offers the possibility to determine the order of the wage costs series independently from the employment data. This can be done straightforwardly by analyzing the bivariate process for wage costs which is assumed to be a simple Markov-process (II.9). In table II.2, the values of three order selection criteria are presented for the wage costs equations in (II.15). Two of them denoted by MSBIC and HKBIC respectively are multivariate variants of Schwarz's univariate Bayesian information criterion. Both criteria yield strongly consistent estimates of the order of the model. The third denoted by LR, is the likelihood-ratio test, which compares the system (2.9) with an autoregressive system with diagonal parameter matrices and one additional lag. Under the null hypothesis, the LR is asymptotically $\chi^2(2)$-distributed. From table II.2 it results for all three criteria that the order of the wage costs series can be chosen to be two. Given the order of the process for wage costs, the order of the wage costs in the equations for employment is completely determined.

Table II.2 : Bivariate order selection tests of (2.9).*

order	MSBIC	HKBIC	LR
1	-3.834	-3.980	--
2	-4.354	-4.649	45.788
3	-4.040	-4.489	0.379
4	-3.739	-4.347	1.584

* The criteria MSBIC and HKBIC are given by Lütkepohl (1984) and Hannan and Kavalieris (1984) respectively. MSBIC= Minimize $(\log|\hat{\Omega}_p|+T^{-1}k^2p \ln T)$; HKBIC= Minimize $(\log|\hat{\Omega}_p|+T^{-1}d(p) \ln T)$, where T is the number of observations, k is the dimension of the process, $\hat{\Omega}_p$ is the ML-estimate of the residual covariance matrix, p is the estimated order of the process and d(p) is the number unknown system parameters.

The determination of the order of the employment process from the data is more difficult. We know that the number of lags in employment in the final model (II.15) is always one more than the order of the stochastic process of s_t in (II.8). This could be checked against the information in the data. We could investigate the order of the four-variate model (II.15). But in absence of computational facilities yet, we assume that the number of lags in the final model (II.15) equals two. Later we will check whether this assumption is in accordance with the sample information. The parameter estimates of (II.15) are obtained from full information maximum likelihood, where V is unknown and updated every iteration according to the Bard-criterium minimizing $|V|$. We used the Davidon- Fletcher-Powell technique to find the maximum of the likelihood function; the parameter τ was chosen a priori to be 0.98. Once the estimates are of (II.15) are obtained, estimates of the structural parameters of both the production function and the adjustment cost function can be computed by asymptotic least squares estimation (ALS).

Table II.3 : Estimation of the restricted model from seasonally adjusted quarterly data 1971.III - 1984.IV (standard errors are given within parentheses).

	blue collar workers				white collar workers		
FIML :	μ_{11}	=	1.245	(0.127)	μ_{21}	=	1.194	(0.216)
	μ_{12}	=	-0.478	(0.150)	μ_{22}	=	-0.431	(0.192)
	ρ_1	=	0.845	(0.082)	ρ_2	=	0.714	(0.168)
	δ_1	=	1.261	(0.824)	δ_2	=	2.680	(2.334)
	λ_4	=	0.373	(0.171)	λ_2	=	0.804	(0.178)
ALS :	α_{12}	=	0.825	(.539)	α_{22}	=	0.381	(0.332)
	β_1	=	0.752	(.430)	β_2	=	6.188	(5.725)

$$\hat{\Sigma} = \begin{bmatrix} .066 & & & \\ .065 & .154 & & \\ -.007 & -.015 & .093 & \\ -.002 & .009 & .019 & .021 \end{bmatrix}$$

log L = 8.747.

Table II.3 shows that the two equations for wage costs satisfy the stability conditions. The fact that the estimate of ρ_1 exceeds that of ρ_2 can be interpreted as a faster reaction of blue collar productivity to exogenous shocks. In other words, blue collar productivity is more flexible. The estimate of the adjustment costs parameter of white collar workers is much higher than that of blue collar workers, a finding that is intuitively plausible. The number of parameters of the restricted model amounts to ten. If we ignore the restrictions on the model (II.15) which are implied by the underlying optimisation model, an unrestricted model with 12 parameters results. To check whether the restrictions are in agreement with the information in the data, we compute the likelihood value of the restricted (L_r) and unrestricted (L_u) models respectively. The associated likelihood ratio statistic equals 3.466. It is asymptotically chi-square distributed with two degrees of freedom, so that we can conclude that the restricted model is in agreement with the sample information.

To see whether the dynamics of the restricted model are correctly specified, we computed the multivariate Box-Pierce (BP) diagnostic test for residual autocorrelation given by Hosking (1980). The BP test has an asymptotic chi-square distribution with 16.s-10 degrees of freedom, where s is the number of autocorrelation matrices on which the test is based, and 10 the number of AR parameters in the model. Results are given in table II.4. The test points out that some autocorrelation occurs in the residuals for lags up to five. Given that the test has little power if s < 10, the conclusion might be justified that no serious residual autocorrelation is left, that could influence the parameter estimates. This aspect has to be further investigated.

Table II.4 : Multivariate Box-Pierce test on residual autocorrelation. *

s	BP	$\chi^2_{.95}$	s	BP	$\chi^2_{.95}$
1	27.86	12.95	6	105.82	108.65
2	54.79	33.92	10	172.54	179.58
3	67.60	53.38	15	255.93	266.38
4	87.11	72.15	20	329.02	352.06
5	97.81	90.53			

* $BP(s) = T^2 \sum_{r=1}^{s} (T-r)^{-1} \; trace \; (\hat{C}'_r \; \hat{C}_0^{-1} \; \hat{C}_r \; \hat{C}_0^{-1});$

where $\hat{C}_r = T^{-1} \sum_{t=r}^{T} \hat{\epsilon}_t \; \hat{\epsilon}'_{t-r} \; .$

More insights into the dynamics of the model can be obtained by analyzing its moving average representation (MAR). For a closed

linear dynamic system the MAR corresponds to the impulse
response function to a unit innovation. The MAR is nonunique.
As we shall see, some response functions have an economic
interpretation. In figures II.1 - II.4 we give the coefficients
of the MAR where the covariance matrix of the innovations of
$(w_{1t}, w_{2t}, n_{1t}, n_{2t})'$ has been diagonalized by a lower triangu-
lar matrix.

The following inference can be drawn from figures II.1 to II.4 :

(i)   A random shock of the wage costs of blue collar workers
       affects the wage costs of blue and white collar workers,
       in almost the same way. This is the result of a positive
       correlation between the two wage costs series.

(ii)   In the short-run, a decrease of the wage costs is paired
       by a rise in the labour demand, and vice versa.

(iii) A positive shock of the wage costs of white collar workers
       has a very small negative effect on the demand for blue
       collar workers and hardly any shortrun effect on the
       demand for white collar workers.

(iv)   A positive random shock in the equation of employment of
       blue collar workers has a long positive effect on both
       sorts of workers. This suggests complementarity of the
       two production factors.

The positive correlation between the two wage costs series can
be explained by institutional factors, like wage-bargaining be-

tween employers and unions. In the industrial sector of the
Netherlands collective wage agreements between employers and
labour unions are negotiated every year for both sorts of
workers. Economic theory gives an explantion for the result
(ii). A fall in prices leads to a rise in demand. The finding
(iii) is due to the difference in quasi-fixedness of both labour
categories. This phenomenon has been observed also in table
II.3, where it is expressed in terms of differences in adjustment cost.

In tables II.5 and II.6, for the various variables in the model
and for the various orders of orthogonalization, we present the
percentage of the forecast error variance accounted for by the
different variables in the model after 40 periods. Table II.5
shows the decomposition of variance implied by the restricted
model (II.15) for parameter estimates which are reported in
table II.3. The variance decomposition in table II.6 is implied
by an unrestricted second order vector autoregression for $(w_{1t}$,
w_{2t}, n_{1t}, $n_{2t})'$. These results are strong evidence for a causal
direction from wage costs to employment, since a considerable
percentage of variance in employment forecasting errors is due
to innovations in real wage costs. There is much less evidence
for causality in the opposite direction. However, a substantial
percentage of variance in forecast errors in employment of one
type of workers can be ascribed to innovations about two types
of labour are dynamically interrelated. The current model does

35

not explicitly account for interaction of production factors, so
that in this respect the model could be further refined.

<u>Table II.5</u> : Percentage forecast error variance decomposition up
to 40-steps-ahead implied by the model (1971.III –
1984.IV).

Orthogonalization	$x\backslash y$	w_1	w_2	n_1	n_2
order: w_1, w_2, n_1, n_2	w_1	100	0	0	0
	w_2	39.5	60.5	0	0
	n_1	25.4	1.4	73.2	0
	n_2	4.8	26.2	17.1	51.9

Orthogonalization	$x\backslash y$	w_1	w_2	n_1	n_2
order: w_2, n_1, n_2, w_1	w_1	57.2	39.5	0	3.3
	w_2	0	100	0	0
	n_1	17.5	8.8	72.7	1.0
	n_2	0	27.9	17.1	55.0

Orthogonalization	$x\backslash y$	w_1	w_2	n_1	n_2
order: n_1, n_2, w_1, w_2	w_1	98.6	0	1.4	0
	w_2	38.1	51.7	3.3	6.9
	n_1	30.2	0	69.8	0
	n_2	6.6	8.9	10.6	73.9

Orthogonalization	$x\backslash y$	w_1	w_2	n_1	n_2
order: n_2, w_1, w_2, n_1	w_1	99.6	0	0	0.4
	w_2	41.1	56.5	0	2.4
	n_1	26.4	4.9	55.2	13.5
	n_2	7.1	9.8	0	83.1

Table II.6 : Percentage forecast error variance decomposition up
to 40-quarters-ahead implied by vector autoregression for (w_1, w_2, n_1, n_2).
(1971.III - 1984.IV).

Orthogonalization	$x\backslash y$	w_1	w_2	n_1	n_2
order: w_1, w_2, n_1, n_2	w_1	83.6	5.0	1.3	10.1
	w_2	72.0	21.0	2.6	4.4
	n_1	38.6	4.4	42.7	14.3
	n_2	4.4	28.8	22.0	44.8
Orthogonalization	$x\backslash y$	w_1	w_2	n_1	n_2
order: w_2, n_1, n_2, w_1	w_1	24.5	62.7	1.3	11.5
	w_2	12.0	80.4	2.6	5.0
	n_1	14.0	27.7	42.7	15.6
	n_2	13.0	17.7	22.1	47.2
Orthogonalization	$x\backslash y$	w_1	w_2	n_1	n_2
order: n_1, n_2, w_1, w_2	w_1	87.1	5.1	1.1	6.6
	w_2	70.8	20.2	4.0	5.0
	n_1	43.3	4.6	42.2	9.8
	n_2	4.9	20.0	21.2	53.9
Orthogonalization	$x\backslash y$	w_1	w_2	n_1	n_2
order: n_2, w_1, w_2, n_1	w_1	83.7	4.9	7.9	3.5
	w_2	72.3	21.4	2.4	3.9
	n_1	38.7	4.4	26.2	30.7
	n_2	4.5	26.5	18.7	50.3

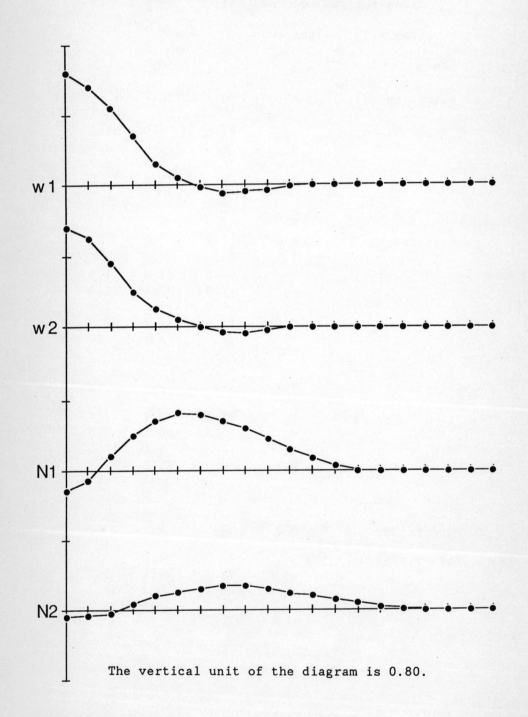

Figure II.1 : Impulse Response of W_1, W_2, N_1, N_2 to Innovation of W_1.

w 1

w 2

N1

N2

The vertical unit of the diagram is 0.80.

Figure II.2 : Impulse Response of W_2, N_1, N_2 to Innovation of W_2.

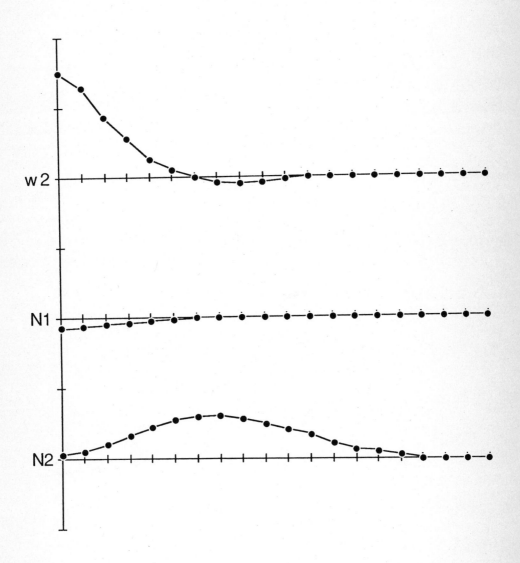

The vertical unit of the diagram is 0.80.

Figure II.3 : Impulse Response of N_1, N_2 to Innovation of N_1.

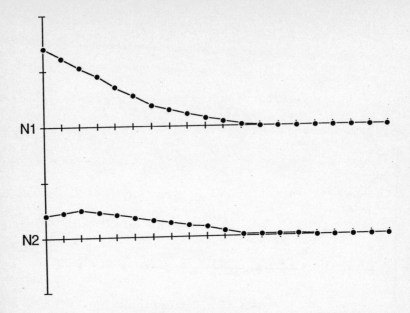

The vertical unit of the diagram is 0.80.

Figure II.4 : Impulse Response of N_2 to Innovation of N_2.

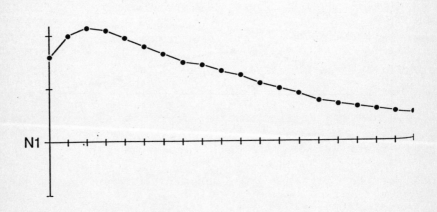

The vertical unit of the diagram is 0.80.

2.5 Conclusions

In chapter 2 we have modeled the dynamic demand for two sorts of labour of firms that are operating under uncertainty in the Dutch manufacturing sector. We modified Sargent's 1978 model of dynamic labour demand. We showed that under the assumption of unidirectional causality of wages to employment it is possible to link the parameter estimates of the model with the structural parameters of a production function and an adjustment cost function.

Our findings can be summarized as follows.

First, white collar labour is a much more quasi-fixed production factor than blue collar labour. In other words, the adjustment costs are much higher for white collar workers than for blue collar workers. This confirms the result found by Nadiri & Rosen (1969) who concluded that the demand for blue collar workers adjusts much more quickly to the desired level than that for employees and for capital goods.

Second, the empirical results suggest a positive correlation between the wage costs of both labour categories, which is the result of the fact that wage bargaining by unions is done for a whole sector or for a single firm. Third, blue and white collar labour seem to be complementary production factors. Employment decisions about the two types of labour have been found to be dynamically interrelated.

Chapter 2 shows that a model based on intertemporal optimization under uncertainty can be used to describe the serial correlation structure of quarterly data on employment and wages in the industry in the Netherlands. The model put forward in this chapter is a prototype model. Several refinements are considered in the following chapters.

CHAPTER 3 : INTERRELATED DEMAND RATIONAL EXPECTATIONS MODELS FOR TWO TYPES OF LABOUR AND PREDETERMINED CAPITAL

3.1 Introduction

A closed form solution (CFS) of a short-run dynamic model of interrelated demand of costly adjustable blue and white collar labour is investigated. Employment decisions are based on rational expectations. The representative firm is assumed to maximize the expected real present value of profits, given the technology and quadratic adjustment costs. Interrelation results from the impact of unpredicted exogenous shocks on the firm's employment policy outcome. This finding is at variance with Nadiri and Rosen (1969) and Meese (1980) who argue that interrelation is due to trade-offs in costs or production.

The theoretical model of the previous chapter is extended modelling interrelated of employment decisions of blue and white collar labour and collar labour and predetermined capital. We obtain interrelation between the two types of labour when the unpredictable components in employment are mutually dependent. Nonstationarity in labour demand is a result of nonstationarity in the forcing variables, wage costs and capital, which are assumed to be given to the firm.

Chapter III is organized as follows, section 2 outlines the extended model. In section 3, the model in CFS is applied to quarterly data of the Dutch manufacturing sector for the period 1971.I - 1984.IV. The structural parameters are estimated using ALS. Interrelation turns out to be essential to appropriately model the dynamics between blue and white collar labour, without previously detrending the data. Moreover, white collar labour appears to be more quasi-fixed and is found to be substitutable for blue collar labour, whereas blue collar labour is complementary with white collar labour. Concluding remarks are given in section 4.

3.2. The Model

A representative firm maximizes its real present value of profits over an infinite time horizon. It employs blue collar workers (n_1), white collar workers (n_2) and uses capital (k).

43

Decisions to change the capital stock are based on costs which are fixed in the short run, and differ materially from short run decisions to change the input of labour. Consequently, the capital stock is assumed to be predetermined. The adjustment of the decision variables of the firm, blue and white collar labour, is costly. The firm operates under uncertainty. In order to determine the optimal level of the variables n_1 and n_2, it uses all the relevant information available up to time t. Current real wage costs are part of the employer's information set.

The firm is assumed to be a price-taker on both factor and output markets. This implies that real wage costs are not Granger-caused by employment. For empirical evidence on unidirectional causality from real wage costs to employment, we refer to Neftçi (1978) and Sargent (1978) for the U.S., to Harris (1985) for the U.K., and to Palm and Pfann (1987) and section 3 of this chapter for the Netherlands.

The production technology obeys the usual regularity conditions ($\partial Y/\partial x_i > 0$, $x = (n_1, n_2, k)$; the Hessian matrix is negative definite) and is locally approximated by a quadratic function

$$(III.1) \quad Y_t(n_{1t}, n_{2t}, k_t) = \sum_{i=1}^{2} \{(\alpha_{i1} + s_{it})n_{it} - \frac{1}{2}\alpha_{i2}n_{it}^2\} +$$

$$+ \alpha_{31}k_t - \frac{1}{2}\alpha_{32}k_t^2 + \alpha_{41}n_{1t}k_t + \alpha_{42}n_{2t}k_t + \alpha_{43}n_{1t}n_{2t}.$$

Y_t denotes the real output per time period, the a_{ij}'s are constant positive parameters. The variables s_{1t} and s_{2t} are exogenous stochastic shocks in the marginal product of labour resulting from changes in the economic environment of the firm.

Rapid adjustment of factor inputs to changes in market conditions can be very costly. Adjustment therefore takes place gradually. In the model, the adjustment costs of labour are assumed to be approximately quadratic. As capital is predetermined, the adjustment costs of capital are not explicitly included in the adjustment cost function. Although it is unlikely that the adjustment cost function is symmetric, for computational ease we use the following adjustment cost function

$$(III.2) \quad AC_t(\Delta_{1t}, \Delta n_{2t}) = \sum_{i=1}^{2} \tfrac{1}{2}\beta_i(\Delta n_{it})^2 + \beta_3 \Delta n_{1t}\Delta n_{2t}.$$

It is worth to emphasize here that Nadiri and Rosen (1969) point out that the existence of dynamically interrelated factor input decisions could be explained by implicit trade-off costs that can occur when a firm follows a mixed strategy of holding inventories of production and hoarding some inputs. Therefore β_3 is expected to be negative. With more specific knowledge required, higher screening and hiring costs, and a longer starting period, it seems plausible that the real costs of adjustment for white collar workers will be higher than those for blue collar workers, i.e. $\beta_2 > \beta_1 > 0$.

The variable cost of factor services are assumed to be as follows

(III.3) $VC_t(n_{1t}, n_{2t}, k_t) = w_{1t}n_{1t} + w_{2t}n_{2t} + c_tk_t,$

where w_{1t}, w_{2t} and c_t denotes real input prices.

Given the capital stock and investment plans, the rational entrepreneur chooses contingency plans for blue and white collar employment. As a consequence of adjustment costs, at time t, the actual employment level and future employment plans have to be determined simultaneously. In the next period, new information forces the firm to revise its employment plans for the future to determine the optimal employment level at time t+1. The firm's objective is to maximize its real present value of profits (PV) at time t, that is

(III.4) $\text{Max } PV_t(n_{1t}, n_{2t}) = \text{Max } E_t \sum_{j=0}^{\infty} \tau^j [Y_{t+j} - AC_{t+j} - VC_{t+j}],$

where b is a real discount factor, $0 < \tau < 1$, and $E_t(.) = E(.|\Omega_t)$, with Ω_t being the available set of information at time t. First order necessary conditions for maximization of (III.4) with respect to the decision variables n_1 and n_2 consists of the set of Euler equations and a pair of transversality conditions which assure the finiteness of the process.

The Euler equations to this infinite time horizon problem can be expressed as follows

(III.5) $bB\ E_t n_{t+1} = An_t - Bn_{t-1} - \Gamma_0 z_t,$

where $n_t = (n_{1t},n_{2t})'$, $z_t = (1,s_{1t},s_{2t},w_{1t},w_{2t},k_t)'$,

$$A = \begin{bmatrix} \alpha_{12} + \beta_1 + \tau\beta_1 & \beta_3 - \alpha_{43} + \tau\beta_3 \\ \beta_3 - \alpha_{43} + \tau\beta_3 & \alpha_{22} + \beta_2 + \tau\beta_2 \end{bmatrix},$$

$$B = \begin{bmatrix} \beta_1 & \beta_3 \\ \beta_3 & \beta_2 \end{bmatrix},$$

$\Gamma_0 = [\ a_1\ \ I_2\ \ -I_2\ \ a_2\ ],$

with $a_1 = (\alpha_{11},\alpha_{21})'$, $a_2 = (\alpha_{41},\alpha_{42})'$ and I_2 the (2x2)-identity matrix.

The planned employment in period t+1 $E_t n_{t+1}$ is linearly related to the current and one period lagged employment level and to the current wage costs and the capital stock. Since $E_t n_{t+1}$ cannot be observed as such it has to be determined within the model. To find a stationary forward looking solution of the Euler linear difference model under rational expectations, that satisfies the transversality conditions we follow Blanchard and Kahn (1980) and transform (III.5) into

(III.6) $E_t\ \mathbb{N}_t = \mathbb{A}\ \mathbb{N}_{t-1} + \mathbb{\Gamma}\ z_t,$

where $\mathbb{N}_t = (n_{1t}, n_{2t}, n_{1t+1}, n_{2t+1})'$;

and $\mathbb{\Gamma} = \begin{bmatrix} 0 \\ \Gamma \end{bmatrix}$ and $\mathbb{A} = \begin{bmatrix} 0 & I_2 \\ -\tau^{-1}I_2 & \tilde{A} \end{bmatrix}$

are (4×2) and (4×4)-matrices respectively with $\Gamma = (\tau B)^{-1}\Gamma_0$ and $\tilde{A} = (\tau B)^{-1}\tilde{A}$. The assumption of $\tilde{A}$ being diagonal implies the absence of mutual dependence in the production process ($\alpha_{43} = 0$) and in the adjustment costs ($\beta_3 = 0$). This "diagonal" model, in which the dynamic demand curves are separable, has been analysed by Sargent (1978) among others. Sargent's model is diagonal for a specific reason, i.e. he distinguishes between straight- and overtime work.

In the sequel of this section, however, we assume $\tilde{A}$ to be a regular (2×2)-matrix. We have the following result.

Proposition 1 : Let $\mathbb{A}$ be the regular matrix as defined in (III.6). Let further $\tilde{A}$ be a regular (2×2)-matrix with eigenvalues μ_1 and μ_2. Then the characteristic polynomial of the matrix $\mathbb{A}$ can be written as

$(-\lambda^2 + \mu_1\lambda - \tau^{-1})(-\lambda^2 + \mu_2\lambda - \tau^{-1})$.

Proof : See Appendix II.

According to proposition 1 the eigenvalues of matrix $\mathbb{A}$ can be found analytically as the roots of a product of two quadratic equations.

48

Proposition 2 : For the quadratic equation $\lambda^2 - \mu\lambda - \delta = 0$ to have one real root λ_a with $|\lambda_a| \leq 1$, and one real root λ_b with $|\lambda_b| > 1$, the following conditions are necessary and sufficient

(i) $\mu^2 + 4\delta \geq 0$

(ii) $(1-\delta)^2 < \mu^2$ or $(1-\delta)^2 = \mu^2$ together with $\delta^2 > 1$.

Proof : Trivial.

If the roots of the characteristics equation of $\mathcal{A}$ satisfy the conditions of proposition 2, the diagonal (4x4)-matrix Λ of eigenvalues of $\mathcal{A}$ can be partitioned as $\Lambda = \begin{bmatrix} \Lambda_1 & 0 \\ 0 & \Lambda_2 \end{bmatrix}$, where

λ_1 is a diagonal matrix with eigenvalues λ_1 and λ_2 smaller than or equal to one in absolute value. The diagonal elements of Λ_2 consist of the eigenvalues λ_3 and λ_4 of $\mathcal{A}$ that lie outside the unit circle. The number of elements of diag (Λ_2) equals the number of stationary forward looking solutions of the difference equation (III.5). When the objective function is quadratic, the number of elements of diag (Λ_1) equals that of diag (Λ_2) (see Hansen and Sargent (1981), Kollintzas (1985)).

The unique stationary forward looking solution of the "diagonal" model yields

(III.7) $n_t = \Lambda_1 n_{t-1} - \sum_{i=0}^{\infty} \Lambda_2^{-i-1} \Gamma E_t \, z_{t+i}$.

Note that $\tau\Lambda_1 = \Lambda_2^{-1}$. The solution is expressed in terms of the eigenvalues of $\tilde{A}$ which are functions of the structural parameters of the underlying theoretical model.

The difference between the "diagonal" model and the model in (III.5) shows up in the dynamic interrelation of labour demand decisions which is explicitly modeled in the latter one.

If $\mu_1 \neq \mu_2$ the matrix A in (III.6) can be transformed such that $\tilde{A}$ is transformed into the diagonal matrix $S^{-1}\tilde{A}S$ with the columns of S being the eigenvectors of $\tilde{A}$. If $\mathbb{C}$ is the matrix of the eigenvectors of $\$^{-1}$ A $\$$ and $\mathbb{C}$ is partitioned according to Λ, we have $\$^{-1}$ A $\$$ = $\mathbb{C}$ Λ $\mathbb{C}^{-1}$ or A = ($\$$ $\mathbb{C}$) Λ ($\$$ $\mathbb{C}$)$^{-1}$, where $\$$, $\mathbb{C}$ and $\mathbb{C}^{-1}$ are (4x4)-matrices decomposed accordingly

$$\$ = \begin{bmatrix} S & 0 \\ 0 & S \end{bmatrix}; \quad \mathbb{C} = \begin{bmatrix} B_{11} & B_{12} \\ B_{21} & B_{22} \end{bmatrix}; \quad \mathbb{C}^{-1} = \begin{bmatrix} C_{11} & C_{12} \\ C_{21} & C_{22} \end{bmatrix}.$$

Now A is written in its Jordan canonical form, where $\tilde{A}$ is diafonalized. The unique stationary forward looking solution of the expected variables in the linear difference equation (III.5) can now be written as follows

(III.8) $\quad n_t = \Lambda_1 n_{t-1} - (SC_{22})^{-1} \sum_{i=0}^{\infty} \Lambda_2^{-i-1} SC_{22} \Gamma E_t z_{t+i}$,

since $-(SC_{22})^{-1}(SC_{21}) = \Lambda_1$.

Expression (III.8) is the CFS of the labour demand equations for an interrelated factor input decision model under uncertainty.

The current employment of blue and white collar workers is linearly related to respectively blue and white collar employment
lagged one period, and the expectations of wage costs, capital
stock and exogenous shocks in productivity over an infinite time
horizon. The parameters of (III.8) are nonlinear functions of
the structural parameters of the theoretical model (III.4).

The finding that Λ_1 in (III.8) is diagonal is remarkable. The
implications of this finding for identification, stability, and
comparative dynamic properties of the model have been thoroughly
discussed by Kollintzas (1985). In the present framework it
means that interrelation between two production factors through
mutual dependence in the production process and in adjustment
costs ($\alpha_{43} \neq 0$, $\beta_3 \neq 0$) does not lead to dynamically interrelated factor demand equations. Therefore, the arguments of Nadiri
and Rosen (1969) concerning the dynamic interrelationship between employment decisions do not apply in the present context.

The second of the right hand side term of (III.8) can be
expressed as

$$(III.9) \quad -(SC_{22})^{-1} \sum_{i=0}^{\infty} \Lambda_2^{-i-1} SC_{22} \Gamma E_t z_{t+i} =$$

$$\delta_0 + \sum_{i=0}^{\infty} H^{-i-1}(\tau B)^{-1} E_t s_{t+i}$$

$$- \sum_{i=0}^{\infty} H^{-i-1}(\tau B)^{-1} E_t w_{t+i}$$

$$+ \sum_{i=0}^{\infty} H^{-i-1}(\tau B)^{-1} a_2 E_t k_{t+i},$$

where $H^{-i-1} = (SC_{22})^{-1} \Lambda_2^{-i-1}(SC_{22})$, and δ_0 is a (2×1)-vector composed of the unconditional means and deterministic fluctuations of marginal labour productivity.

Now we make assumptions on the stochastic properties of the forcing variables s_t, w_t and k_t. The stochastic components of labour productivity s_t are assumed to be generated by a stationary first order Markov process $E_t s_{t+1} = \tilde{R} s_t$, where $\tilde{R}$ is a (2×2)-matrix. Let Q_s be a (2×2)-matrix, such that $Q_s s_t$ is a stationary AR(1) process with innovation ξ^s_t

(III.10) $Q_s s_t = RQ_s s_{t-1} + \xi^s_t$,

where $R = Q_s \tilde{R} Q_s^{-1}$, is a stationary (2×2)-matrix.

$\underline{\text{Proposition 3}}$: Let $Q_s = \sum\limits_{i=0}^{\infty} (SC_{22})^{-1} \Lambda_2^{-i-1} SC_{22}(\tau B)^{-1}\tilde{R}^i$. Then

$vec(Q_s) = [I_2 \otimes [(SC_{22})^{-1} \Lambda_2 SC_{22}] - \tilde{R}^T \otimes I_2]^{-1} vec((\tau B)^{-1})$.

$\underline{\text{Proof}}$: See Appendix II.

The results of proposition 3 enable us to find an explicit solution of $\sum\limits_{i=1}^{\infty} H^{-i-1}(\tau B)^{-1} E_t s_{t+i}$ in terms of the structural parameters.

In accordance with the literature on dynamic labour demand, real wage costs are assumed to be generated by a bivariate autoregressive process. The order of the process has been

determined prior to estimation of the model in CFS. A justifi-
cation of the prior analysis is given in the next section; w_t is
described by a bivariate second order autoregression

(III.11) $w_t = \delta_w + M_1 w_{t-1} + M_2 w_{t-2} + \xi_t^w,$

where δ_w is a (2×1)-vector of constants, M_1 and M_2 are
(2×2)-matrices and ξ_t^w is a (2×1)-vector of innovations of the
wage costs. The second r.h.s. term of (III.9) becomes

$$\sum_{i=0}^{\infty} H^{-i-1}(\tau B)^{-1} E_t w_{t+i} = P_1 w_1 + P_2 w_{t-1}$$

with $P_1 + H^{-1}(\tau B)^{-1}V$ and $P_2 = H^{-2}(\tau B)^{-1}V M_2$, where V is a
(2×2)-matrix such that $HVM_1 + H^2VM_2 = I_2$.

Finally, empirical evidence that will be presented in the next
section shows that the first difference of the predetermined
capital stock can be represented as a random walk with drift

(III.12) $\Delta k_t = \delta_k + \xi_t^k.$

Hence, an explicit solution for the third r.h.s. term in (III.9)
is

$(H - I_2)^{-1}(bB)^{-1} a_2 k_t.$

Elimination of the autocorrelation of $Q_s s_t$ is achieved using a
Koyck transformation.   We substitute the expressions for the
expected values of s_t, w_t and k_t into (III.8)′, assuming that

the lagged values of the forcing variables are not correlated with the composite disturbance term ξ_t^n.

Applying proposition 3, the reduced form of the labour demand equations becomes

$$(\text{III}.13) \quad n_t = \delta + (\Lambda_1 + R)n_{t-1} - R\Lambda_1 n_{t-2} + Ck_{t-1}$$

$$+ (P_1 M_1 - RP_1 + P_2)w_{t-1} + (P_1 M_2 - RP_2)w_{t-2} + \xi_t^n,$$

where $C = (I_2 - R)(H - I_2)^{-1}(\tau B)^{-1}a_2$, $\delta = \delta(\delta_0, \delta_w, \delta_k)$, and $\xi_t^n = \xi_t^n(\xi_t^s, \xi_t^w, \xi_t^k)$.

Labour demand innovations, ξ_t^n, is linearly related to unanticipated changes in labour productivity (ξ_t^s), wage costs (ξ_t^w) and capital (ξ_t^k). From (III.13) it follows that dynamic interrelation in the autoregressive part of the employment equations can only result from the serial cross-correlation in the exogenous productivity shocks. Or, stated more formally, when the objective function is quadratic, interrelation between decisions on the current level of employment of blue and white collar workers occurs if and only if the matrix R of the process for the stochastic components of labour productivity is nondiagonal. If R is a diagonal matrix, both labour demand equations are dynamically interrelated via the capital stock and the wages only. Consequently, the assumption in Meese (1980) of marginal labour productivity being white noise implies that the parameters of interrelation in the reduced form equations can not be identified.

The system of equations (III.11) and (III.13) yields a complete linear multivariate model which can be empirically analysed. The disturbance term $(\xi_t^w, \xi_t^n)'$ is assumed to be normally distributed with mean zero and covariance matrix Σ, which, as a result of the mutual influences of unanticipated exogenous movements of productivity, wage costs, and capital, is assumed to be unrestricted except for symmetry and positive definiteness.

3.3 An Empirical Analysis

In this section we apply the model for interrelated labour demand in CFS to quarterly data of the Dutch manufacturing sector for the period 1971.I to 1984.IV. All series are seasonally unadjusted. The data are obtained from the Central Bureau of Statistics and the Central Planning Bureau. A description of the series and the data are given in Appendix I. Labour demand has been disaggregated into the demand for blue and white collar labour, both expressed in terms of working hours times the number of workers for each category respectively. The effects of possible substitution between hours worked and persons employed has not been taken into account.

Prior to the econometric analysis of labour demand equations, we have tested for Granger causality between wage costs and employment. Possible causal relations between wage costs and employment were examined separately for each sort of labour by means of a bivariate AR(4)-model, ignoring the possible influences of other time series. The chi-square values of leaving four lags of employment out of the wage costs equation were 5.56 and 7.46 (p-values .24 and .12) for blue and white collar labour respectively.

Leaving the four lags of wage costs out of the employment equation yielded chi-square values of 16.80 and 11.18 (p-values .00 and .02) respectively. Consequently, the hypothesis of unidirectional causality from real wage costs to employment is found to be in accordance with the empirical evidence when each type of labour is considered separately. When we consider blue and white collar labour simultaneously we also find stronger evidence in favour of the unidirectional relationship. However, the significance of these tests is not so clear-cut. Chi-square values for joint causality tests with 16 degrees of freedom on a four variate AR(4) model for the four series amounted to 29.97 (p-value .02) when unidirectional causality from wage costs to employment is tested, and 47.59 (p-value .00) when unidirectional causality of employment to wage costs is analysed.

The unidirectional causality assumption enables us to model the dynamic interactions between real wage costs and employment along the lines outlined in the previous section. Moreover, then the wage costs equations can be analysed independently from the employment data. Fuller's τ_τ statistic testing for unit roots in w_{1t} and w_{2t} applied to an AR(2) model with constant term yield -1.27 ($\overline{R}^2 = 0.99$) and -2.09 ($\overline{R}^2 = 0.99$), which does not lead to the rejection of the hypothesis of a unit root in both cases.

Bivariate identification of the wage costs series has been carried out by means of a computer package provided by Liu et al. (1986). The results for the first differences of the cost series are presented in Table III.2. First differencing yields stationary wage series. Standard errors (s.e.) are given between parentheses. Stationary vector time series can be usefully described by their cross correlation (CCM) (see for further details e.g. Tiao and Box (1981)). The χ^2-test for the lag length, and the Akaike Information Criteria (AIC) can be used to determine the order of an autoregressive model.

The CCMs of Δw_t cut off after one lag. The χ^2-statistic and AIC suggest an AR(1) process. Since after one lag the autocorrelations of Δw_{1t} and Δw_{2t} die out and their partial autocorrelations equal zero, we tentatively select a bivariate AR(1) process for Δw_t with a diagonal first order autoregressive parameter matrix.

On the basis of the empirical findings, the model (III.11) becomes

<u>Table III.2</u> : Identification of the Wage Costs Series.

I : BIVARIATE IDENTIFICATION OF $\Delta w_t = \Delta(w_{1t}, w_{2t})'$

The Cross Correlation Matrices of Δw_t

lag	1	2	3	4	5	6
CCM	.42* .40*	.13 .14	.04 .18	-.10 .07	-.09 -.16	-.14 -.20
	.41* .53*	.19 .26	.06 .17	-.01 .04	-.05 -.13	-.15 -.24

Criteria for Autoregressive Order Identification

lag	1	2	3	4	5	6
CHI(4)	18.21	1.90	5.94	2.59	3.23	1.85
AIC	-5.887	-5.788	-5.788	-5.711	-5.654	-5.564

II : UNIVARIATE ORDER SELECTION

Autocorrelations of Univariate Series

Δw_{1t} [mean = .143 (.285)]

lag	1	2	3	4	5	6	7	8
AC	.419	.125	.032	.109	-.081	-.143	-.027	-.047
s.e.	(.137)	(.160)	(.162)	(.162)	(.163)	(.164)	(.166)	(.166)

Δw_{2t} [mean = . 234 (.460)]

lag	1	2	3	4	5	6	7	8
AC	.528	.252	.162	.017	-.156	-.250	-.254	-.113
s.e.	(.137)	(.171)	(.178)	(.181)	(.181)	(.184)	(.190)	(.196)

Partial Autocorrelations of Univariate Series

Δw_{1t} [s.e. = .137]

lag	1	2	3	4	5	6	7	8
PA	.950	-.057	-.006	-.078	-.062	-.036	-.006	-.030

Δw_{2t} [s.e. = .137]

lag	1	2	3	4	5	6	7	8
PA	.528	.037	.061	-.120	-.172	-.126	-.058	.136

"*" larger than $2n^{-\frac{1}{2}}$, where n denotes the number of observations.

(III.11)' $\quad w_t = (I + M)w_{t-1} - Mw_{t-2} + \xi_t^w$,

with $M = \text{diag}(m_1, m_2)$.

Fuller's τ_τ statistic testing for a unit root in k_t applied to an AR(1) process with constant term yields -0.16 ($\bar{R}^2 = 0.99$). Therefore, we assume that Δk_t follows a random walk with drift, which leads to the explicit solution of the infinite future expectations of capital as presented in the previous section.

Consequently, the reduced form employment equations fitted to the data are as follows

(III.13)' $\quad n_t = \delta(\text{CONST}, Q2, Q3, Q4) + (\Lambda_1 + R)n_{t-1} - R\Lambda_1 n_{t-2}$

$\quad\quad\quad + Ck_{t-1} + (P_1[I+M] - RP_1 + P_2)w_{t-1} - (P_1M + RP_2)w_{t-2} + \xi_t^w$,

where R is a nondiagonal (2×2)-matrix and Q2, Q3, Q4 denote seasonal dummies for the second, third and fourth quarter, respectively.

The identified structural parameters of the model presented in section 2 are estimated using a two step estimation procedure proposed by Chamberlain (1982) and Gouriéroux et al. (1985). In a first stage, an unrestricted version of the reduced form of the model is estimated that incorporates the restrictions on the order of the system implied by the underlying theory. This model, that will be referred to as model 1, is equivalent to the

59

Table III.3a : Maximum Likelihood Estimates of the Unrestricted Model 1 *.

	Blue Collar Workers			White Collar Workers		
Wage Costs	$m_1 = 0.44$	(5.48)		$m_2 = 0.58$	(4.25)	
Employment	$n_{1t-1} =$	1.27	(8.75)	$n_{1t-1} =$	-0.10	(-1.42)
	$n_{1t-2} =$	-0.29	(-2.70)	$n_{1t-2} =$	0.16	(3.06)
	$n_{2t-1} =$	-1.12	(-3.47)	$n_{2t-1} =$	1.22	(7.69)
	$n_{2t-2} =$	0.99	(2.89)	$n_{2t-2} =$	-0.28	(-1.64)
	$w_{1t-1} =$	-0.13	(-1.64)	$w_{1t-1} =$	-0.06	(-1.50)
	$w_{1t-2} =$	0.07	(0.88)	$w_{1t-2} =$	0.001	(0.37)
	$w_{2t-1} =$	-0.09	(-1.50)	$w_{2t-1} =$	-0.002	(-0.70)
	$w_{2t-2} =$	0.16	(2.73)	$w_{2t-2} =$	0.07	(2.57)
	$k_{t-1} =$	-0.03	(-1.31)	$k_{t-1} =$	0.01	(0.54)

* Asymptotic t-values are given within parentheses. The estimated coefficients of constants and seasonal dummies are not reported in the table.

Table III.3b : Asymptotic Least Squares Structural Parameter Estimates when $\beta_3 = 0$, $\alpha_{43} = 0$, and $\tau = 0.98$ *.

	Blue Collar Workers			White Collar Workers		
Wage Costs	m_1	= 0.48	(4.98)	m_2	= 0.53	(3.83)
Technology	α_{12}	= 1.08	(2.61)	α_{22}	= 1.17	(2.40)
	α_{41}	= 0.41	(1.49)	α_{42}	= 0.20	(1.12)
Adjustment Costs	β_1	= 34.31	(5.89)	β_2	= 85.07	(4.31)
Serial Correlation R of Productivity Shocks	ρ_{11}	= 0.51	(2.40)	ρ_{12}	= -0.81	(-1.59)
	ρ_{21}	= -0.10	(-0.84)	ρ_{22}	= 0.62	(1.92)

* Asymptotic t-values are given within parentheses.

model of (III.11)' and (III.13)' in which the autoregressive matrices $\Lambda_1 + R$, $R\Lambda_1$, $P_1[I+M] - RP_1 + P_2$ and $P_1 M + RP_2$ are assumed to be unrestricted nondiagonal (2×2)-matrices, and C is a (2×1)-vector of unrestricted parameters. Parameter estimates of model 1 are obtained by maximum likelihood, and are given in table III.3a. In the second stage, the structural parameters are estimated using the method of Asymptotic Least Squares (ALS) which minimizes the distance between the unrestricted reduced form estimates and the reduced form coefficients expressed as functions of the identified structural parameters. The ALS procedure is asymptotically equivalent to Maximum Likelihood (ML) estimation methods, provided ML estimates of the parameter estimates from the first stage are used together with an optimal weighting matrix and all restrictions between structural parameters and reduced form coefficients have been imposed. In order to obtain the weighting matrix the derivatives of the nonlinear relationships between the parameters estimated in the first stage and the structural parameters are needed.

Since the capital stock is assumed to be predetermined (in the short run), the technology parameters α_{31} and α_{32} in (III.1) are not identified; α_{43} and β_3 are not identified separately either. We impose the prior restrictions $\beta_3 = 0$ and $\alpha_{43} = 0$; the parameter τ was chosen a priori to be 0.98 for quarterly data. ALS estimates of α_{12}, α_{22}, α_{41}, α_{42}, β_1, β_2, and the elements of the (2x2)-matrices R and M are obtained from the set of implicit relationships relating the 20 parameter estimates of the unrestricted model 1 to the 12 structural parameters of the model in CFS. Estimation results are given in table III.3b.

As a byproduct, we computed a WALD statistic testing the appropriateness of the overidentifying restrictions imposed by the underlying theory. We compare the model of the form of (III.11)' and (III.13)' in which all the parameters are functions of the 12 structural parameters with model 1. (We abstract from the parameters of the seasonal dummies which have been included in both models). The test, which is equivalent to the standard LR test on overidentifying restrictions, is asymptotically $\chi^2(8)$-distributed and yields a value of 10.80 (p-value 0.22).

The estimates of the serial correlation matrix R can be interpreted as measures of the speed of adjustment of productivity of both types of labour to unforeseen productivity shocks. For instance, a positive shock in product demand implying an increase in ξ_t^s is initially absorbed by a large change of blue collar productivity compared with that of white collar labour, in such a way that the discounted effect of both types of labour productivity is positive. This result is a first indication that blue collar labour is more flexibly

adjusted than white collar labour. The estimates of the adjustment costs parameters β_1 and β_2 indicate that white collar
labour is more quasi-fixed than blue collar labour. Since the
hiring procedure will be more expensive, and white collar
workers is expected to need more job-specific training, it is
plausible that the costs of adjustment (hiring and/or firing)
will be much higher for white collar labour than for blue collar
labour.

The technology parameters are found to be positive. These findings are in agreement with the assumptions underlying the
theoretical model, i.e. technology, adjustment costs and the
process for productivity shocks are specified such that the
optimality conditions (concavity of production technology, convexity of adjustment costs, both locally approximated using
quadratic shapes, and stationarity of productivity shocks) are
satisfied.

Using proposition 1 and the structural parameter estimates from
table 3 we can compute $\lambda_1 = 0.85$ and $\lambda_2 = 0.90$, and the eigen-
values of $\tilde{A}$, sc. $\mu_1 = (\tau^{-1} + \lambda_1^2)/\lambda_1 = 2.05$ and $\mu_2 = (\tau^{-1} + \lambda_2^2)/$
$\lambda_2 = 2.03$. Both the eigenvalues satisfy the necessary and suf-
ficient conditions of proposition 2. Moreover, the estimates of
the diagonal elements of Λ_2, $\lambda_3 = \frac{1}{2}(\mu_1 + \sqrt{\mu_1^2 - 4/\tau}) = 1.20$ and
$\lambda_4 = \frac{1}{2}(\mu_2 + \sqrt{\mu_2^2 - 4/\tau}) = 1.14$ lie outside the unit circle.

63

In addition, we compute a LR test comparing model 1 with less complex separate dynamic wage and employment curves. The model with separate demand curves will be referred to as model 2, and is equivalent to the model of (III.11)' and (III.13)' in which the autoregressive matrices Λ_1+R, $R\Lambda_1$, $P_1[I+M]-RP_1+P_2$ and P_1M+RP_2 are assumed to be unrestricted diagonal matrices and C is a (2x1)-vector of unrestricted parameters. The LR test is asymptotically $\chi^2(8)$-distributed and yields a value of 42.20 (p-value 0.00).

The multivariate portmanteau test suggested by Hosking (1980) is a consistent LM statistic for residual autocorrelation. Table III.4 contains LM tests for the model (III.11)', (III.13)' for model 1, being the unrestricted version of the model with inter-related employment equations in CFS, and for model 2. The LM test has an asymptotic chi-squared distribution with degrees of freedom that depend on s, the order of autocorrelated lags, the dimension of the model (4), and the number of estimated autoregressive parameters.

From Table III.4 we see that the inclusion of interrelation in labour demand decisions removes the lower order residual auto-correlation. On the whole, we find that the interrelated model is superior to the diagonal model. To summarize, we may conclude that dynamic interrelation between the demand of blue and white collar labour is probably the result of the serial correlation of productivity shocks, and that the inclusion of interrelations between the two types of labour demand has improved the model significantly. The overidentifying restrictions of the rational expectations model, implied by underlying economic theory do seem to be corroborated by the sample evidence.

Table III.4 : Multivariate Lagrange Multiplier Tests on Residual Autocorrelation.

s	Equations (III.11)' (III.13)'		Model 1		Model 2	
	LM	$\chi^2(.95)$	LM	$\chi^2(.95)$	LM	$\chi^2(.95)$
3	40.19	46.19	37.22	43.77	53.93	48.60
4	56.96	65.17	52.45	62.83	66.85	67.51
5	66.64	83.68	61.37	81.38	82.09	85.97
10	119.52	173.00	124.15	170.81	139.46	175.20
15	210.76	259.92	206.62	257.61	241.03	262.07
20	293.02	345.67	280.08	343.53	322.08	347.80

In order to get a better insight into the dynamic properties of the model we compute a moving average representation in terms of orthogonal disturbances of the model in CFS. Figure III.1 shows the impulse responses of the demand for blue and white collar labour to a unit innovation of blue and white collar employment respectively. The impulse response traces out the reaction of a firm to uncorrelated shocks in the two demand functions. We note that ξ^n is a linear combination of ξ^s, ξ^w, ξ^k, such that a positive unit innovation in ξ^n can be interpreted as a positive shock in labour productivity or capital, or as a negative shock in real wage costs.

The impulse responses to innovations of labour input differ between the two types. A positive shock in the demand for blue collar workers lead to a rise in the employment of blue as well as white collar labour. The estimated response of n_1 is stronger but shorter, while the estimated response of n_2 is more moderate but lasts longer due to higher adjustment costs. This result could be interpreted as follows. The impact of a shock damps out very quickly with employment returning to its original level. Conversely, if the hiring of white collar labour is costly, the adjustment to a shock negatively affects employment of blue collar workers. This leads to the conclusion that on the one hand white collar labour is complementary to blue collar labour. When more workers are hired, more supervisors will be needed. On the other hand, a single upswing in white collar labour demand leads to a displacement effect on the employment of blue collar workers. The firm's work force is upgraded.

Blue collar labour can be substituted by white collar labour.

Figure III.1 : Impulse response of n_1 and n_2 to innovations in ξ^{n1} and ξ^{n2}.

The Impulse response of n_1 to innovations in ξ^{n1}

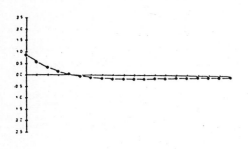

Impulse response of n_2 to innovations in ξ^{n1}

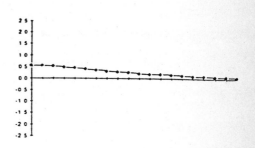

The Impulse response of n_1 to innovations in ξ^{n2}

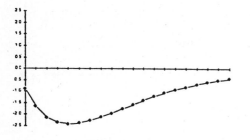

Impulse response of n_2 to innovations in ξ^{n2}

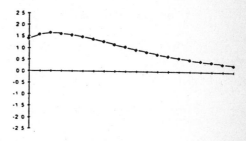

3.4 Conclusions

In the present chapter the relation between the parameters of the econometric model and the structural parameters have been derived. Although these relationships are highly nonlinear, the structural parameters, which have an economic interpretation can be estimated. The adjustment costs and productivity of the two types of labour were assumed to be interrelated. We showed that when an employer maximizes a quadratic objective function, interrelation of the two decision variables does not emerge from interrelated mutual dependence in the production process. Costs trade offs do not lead to interrelation in the labour demand equations either. In a rational expectations framework with quadratic objective function, interrelation of employment decisions can only result from the interdependence of the exogenous shocks in the firm's economic environment.

Application of the model to analyse labour demand schedules of the Dutch manufacturing sector showed that interrelation is in accordance with the sample data. An earlier finding by e.g. Nadiri and Rosen (1969), that white collar labour is more quasi-fixed than blue collar labour due to higher adjustment costs is confirmed by this research. The moving average representation of the labour demand equations of the estimated model showed that the number of blue collar workers employed cannot be increased without raising the number of white collar workers employed. On the other hand, a single upswing in white collar labour demand has a displacement effect on blue collar workers employment. Therefore it can be stated that blue collar labour is complementary with white collar labour, whereas white collar labour is substitutable for blue collar labour in the Dutch manufacturing sector.

The present model can easily be extended to include more than two interrelated inputs. For instance, the capital stock can be introduced as a decision variable. Application of such a model is expected to give more insights into the relation between quasi-fixed white collar labour and the capital stock, which is fixed in the short-run.

Matters concerned with the adjustment of labour input and the flexibility of working hours in reaction to unforeseen shocks in the environment of the firm are not considered either. Another interesting subject of analysis is concerned with the stability of the firm's decision rule when expectations are rational. Do all the parameters of this process remain unchanged when a shift in product demand of factor prices occurs which was not antici-pated? To put it differently, does the firm interpret an unex-pected change in its environment as an innovation or as a struc-tural change in the process generating the exogenous variables? These questions will be addressed in the next chapter.

CHAPTER 4 : EXOGENOUS SHOCKS AND COINTEGRATION IN MULTIVARIATE
FLEXIBLE ACCELERATOR MODELS OF LABOUR AND CAPITAL

4.1 Introduction

This chapter is concerned with dynamic factor demand systems.
First, the solution of the stochastic control problem, applied
in chapter 3 for the examination of a bivariate labour demand
model with capital being predetermined, is used in this chapter
to get more insights into the restrictions on the parameters of
multivariate flexible accelerator models in which capital and
labour are determined simultaneously. Second, in line with the
Lucas critique, the impact of a structural change in the process
of the exogenous variables for the factor demand is analysed.
Third, the nonstationarity of the factor demand series can be
accounted for by the nonstationarity in the relative factor prices when the demand and price series are cointegrated.

The plan of chapter four is as follows. Section 2 describes the
theoretical model and gives a closed-form solution for the
linear rational expectations factor demand model. The impact of
both temporary innovations and structural changes in the process
of the exogenous variables on factor demand is discussed.
Section 3 contains an empirical analysis of the Dutch manufacturing sector for the period 1971.I - 1984.IV. Capital and
labour are found to be cointegrated with the real price of

assets and real labor costs. The model is estimated using a two step estimation procedure which is asymptotically equivalent to maximum likelihood (ML) estimation. The impacts of the oil price shocks in 1973.IV and 1979.II are modelled as a structural change in the process of the exogenous variables. This approach leads to an improvement of the model. Section 4 concludes this chapter.

4.2 The Model and Its Solution

A representative firm produces output y using an 2n-vector of inputs $x = (\ell',k')'$, where ℓ is an n-vector of employment and k is an n-vector of capital stocks depreciating through time. At time t, the production function of the firm is defined as

$$y_t = y(x_t,s_t) = (\alpha + s_t)'x_t - \tfrac{1}{2}x_t'Ax_t, \tag{IV.1}$$

where α is a 2n-vector of positive constant parameters, A is a symmetric, positive definite (2n×2n)-matrix and s_t is a 2n-vector of exogenous stochastic shocks of the production technology.

When the firm wants to alter the factor inputs, it faces adjustment costs which reflect the quasi-fixedness of inputs. Costs of search, training, market research, reorganization are examples of adjustment costs of factor inputs. The adjustment cost function, ac, is given by

71

$$ac_t = ac(\Delta x_t) = \tfrac{1}{2}\Delta x_t' B \Delta x_t, \qquad (IV.2)$$

where Δ is the difference operator, B is a regular $(2n \times 2n)$-matrix with off-diagonal elements reflecting the trade-off of costs resulting when several inputs are altered simultaneously. The variable costs, vc, consist of wage and investment costs

$$vc_t = vc(x_t, w_t, q_t) = w_t' \ell_t + q_t'(k_t - (I-\delta)k_{t-1}), \qquad (IV.3)$$

where w_t and q_t are n-vectors of stochastic real labor costs and real prices of investment goods respectively and δ denotes a diagonal $(n \times n)$-matrix with constant depreciation rates on its diagonal. All prices are normalized by the price of output and assumed to be given to the firm.

The firm's objective is to maximize its real present value of profits, that is

$$\underset{\ell, k}{\text{maximize}} \ E \left[\sum_{i=0}^{\infty} \tau^i (y_{t+i} - ac_{t+i} - vc_{t+i}) \ \Big| \ \Omega_t \right], \qquad (IV.4)$$

where Ω_t is the information set available to the firm at time t, and τ is a constant real discount factor. At each period t, the firm chooses contingency plans for ℓ and k, by solving the first order conditions

$$E[x_{t+1}|\Omega_t] = -(\tau B)^{-1}\alpha + ((1+\tau^{-1})I + (\tau B)^{-1}A)x_t - \tau^{-1}x_{t-1}$$
$$-(\tau B)^{-1}s_t + (\tau B)^{-1}p_t - (\tau B)^{-1}dE[p_{t+1}|\Omega_t], \qquad (IV.5)$$

where I is the $(2n \times 2n)$-identity matrix, $p_t = (w_t', q_t')'$ and d is a diagonal $(2n \times 2n)$-matrix $\begin{bmatrix} 0 & 0 \\ 0 & \tau(I-\delta) \end{bmatrix}$. We can rewrite (IV.5) as follows

$$\begin{bmatrix} x_t \\ E[x_{t+1}|\Omega_t] \end{bmatrix} = \begin{bmatrix} 0 & I \\ -\tau^{-1}I & \tilde{A} \end{bmatrix} \begin{bmatrix} x_{t-1} \\ x_t \end{bmatrix} + \begin{bmatrix} 0 \\ (\tau B)^{-1} z_t \end{bmatrix}, \quad (IV.6)$$

where $\tilde{A} = ((1+\tau^{-1})I + (\tau B)^{-1}A)$ and $z_t = -\alpha - s_t + p_t - dE[p_{t+1}|\Omega_t]$.

Hansen and Sargent (1981) have proved that for a quadratic objective function the number of stationary solutions to (IV.5) is equal to the number of non-stationary solutions. Kollintzas (1985) generalized this finding, proving that a multivariate symmetric adjustment costs model has structural parameters that are real.

If $\tilde{A}$ has 2n eigenvalues stored in two diagonal $(n \times n)$-matrices M_1 and M_2, then the characteristic equation associated with (IV.6) becomes

$$(-\Lambda^2 + M_1\Lambda - \tau^{-1}I)(-\Lambda^2 + M_2\Lambda - \tau^{-1}I) = 0. \quad (IV.7)$$

If all the eigenvalues of $\tilde{A}$ differ, then a unique stationary forward looking solution of the linear difference equation set (IV.5) exists (see Blanchard and Kahn (1980), and chapter 3 of this dissertation)

$$x_t = \Lambda_1 x_{t-1} - C^{-1} \sum_{i=0}^{\infty} (\Lambda_2)^{-i-1} C(\tau B)^{-1} E[z_{t+i}|\Omega_t], \qquad (IV.8)$$

where Λ_2 is a diagonal $(2n \times 2n)$-matrix of solutions of $(IV.7)$ which are greater than one in absolute value, and Λ_1 is a diagonal $(2n \times 2n)$-matrix that contains the eigenvalues of $(IV.7)$ that do not lie outside the unit circle.

We note that $\Lambda_1 \Lambda_2 = \tau^{-1} I$, according to $(IV.7)$. If $\tilde{A}$ and Λ_1 are partitioned as follows :

$$\tilde{A} = \begin{bmatrix} A_{11} & A_{12} \\ A_{21} & A_{22} \end{bmatrix}, \text{ and } \Lambda_1 = \begin{bmatrix} \Lambda_{11} & 0 \\ 0 & \Lambda_{12} \end{bmatrix}, \text{ then}$$

$$C = \begin{bmatrix} A_{12} & A_{12} \\ M_1 - A_{11} & M_2 - A_{11} \end{bmatrix} \begin{bmatrix} \tau\Lambda_{11}(\tau\Lambda_{11}^2 - I)^{-1} & 0 \\ 0 & \tau\Lambda_{12}(\tau\Lambda_{12}^2 - I)^{-1} \end{bmatrix},$$

where all submatrices are of order $n \times n$.

By definition the autoregressive part of $(IV.8)$ is stationary. This important restriction implies that a non-stationarity of factor inputs arises through current and expected future levels of the exogenous variables, such as factor prices.

In the multivariate flexible accelerator type models (e.g. Treadway (1971) and Epstein and Denny (1983)), the interrelated adjustment path for factor inputs, is as follows

$$\Delta x_t = M(x_{t-1} - x^*), \qquad (IV.9)$$

where x^* is a steady state equilibrium and M denotes a stable adjustment matrix of order 2n. However, from (IV.8) we get that I+M = Λ_1, which implies that M must be diagonal if the structural model is quadratic. We note that Epstein and Yatchew (1985), hereafter denoted as EY, argue that M has 2n eigenvalues lying between -1 and 0.

EY solve a deterministic (certainty equivalence) version of (IV.4) replacing all random variables by their conditional expected values. EY "avoid the difficulty of solving" (IV.4) (p.240) to find the closed form solution (IV.5) with Λ_1 (= I+M in EY) expressed as a function of α, A and B, by reparametrizing the production function f in terms of α, B and Λ_1.

This technique, however, cannot be applied if f contains a multiplicative disturbance term $s_t x_t$ as in (IV.1). Moreover, by reparametrizing, information on Λ_1 is lost which appears to be crucial when modeling interrelated factor demand given a quadratic objective function, since Λ_1 is diagonal. Although none of structural parameter matrices, A and B, were assumed to be diagonal, we find that independently from assumptions on expectations formations processes the adjustment matrix is diagonal. EY estimate P = BM, assuming B is diagonal. Consequently, P is diagonal, which is confirmed by the empirical results of EY, where unrestricted estimates of the off-diagonal parameter P_2 of the symmetric matrix P are -.001 and 0.00000 respectively for different periods (see EY, table 5, p. 249).

In order to derive explicit factor input decision rules we specify the stochastic processes, s_t and p_t. Stochastic movements
of factor productivity are assumed to follow a stationary first
order Markov process $E[s_{t+i}|\Omega_t] = \tilde{R}^i s_t$, where $\tilde{R}$ is a
(2n×2n)-matrix. Let S be a (2n×2n)-matrix, such that S s_t is a
stationary AR(1) process with innovation ξ_t^s

$$S\ s_t = RS\ s_{t-1} + \xi_t^s, \qquad (IV.10)$$

where R is a (2n×2n)-matrix satisfying the stability conditions
and let

$$vec(S) = (I \ominus C^{-1}(\tau\Lambda_1)^{-1}C - \tilde{R}' \ominus I)^{-1}\ vec((\tau B)^{-1})$$

then

$$C^{-1} \sum_{i=0}^{\infty} (\tau\Lambda_1)^{i+1}\ C(\tau B)^{-1}\ E[s_{t+i}|\Omega_t] = S\ s_t. \qquad (IV.11)$$

The proof of this result is fairly straightforward and is given
in chapter three.

The stochastic process for p_t is assumed to be an autoregressive
process of order q :

$$p_t = c^p + Q_1 p_{t-1} + Q_2 p_{t-2} + \cdots + Q_p p_{t-q} + \xi_t^p, \qquad (IV.12)$$

where c^p is a 2n-vector of constants, Q_1 to Q_q are (2n×2n)-
matrices of constant parameters and ξ_t^p is the innovation of prices. Then

$$c^{-1} \sum_{i=0}^{\infty} (\tau\Lambda_1)^{i+1} \, C(\tau B)^{-1} E[p_{t+i} - d p_{t+i+1} | \Omega_t] = \tilde{c}^p + \tilde{Q}_0 p_t + \tilde{Q}_1 p_{t-1}$$
$$+ \ldots + \tilde{Q}_{q-1} p_{t-q+1}, \qquad (IV.13)$$

where $\tilde{c}^p = c^{-1}((\tau\Lambda_1)^{-1} - I)^{-1} \, C((\tau B)^{-1} - (\tau B)^{-1} d) c^p$,

$\quad \tilde{Q}_0 = c^{-1} \, \Lambda_1 \, C B^{-1} v$,

$\quad \tilde{Q}_i = \sum_{j=2}^{q-i+1} (c^{-1}(\tau\Lambda_1)^{j-1} C)(c^{-1}\Lambda_1 C B^{-1} - (\tau B)^{-1} d) V Q_{j+i-1}$;

$\quad i = 1, \ldots, q-1$

and where V is a $(2n \times 2n)$-matrix such that $\sum_{j=1}^{q} c^{-1}(\tau\Lambda_1)^j \, C V Q_j = I$.

Substituting (IV.11), (IV.12) and (IV.13) into (IV.8), and applying a Koyck transformation to eliminate the autocorrelation in (IV.10), the reduced form of the factor demand equations becomes

$$x_t = c^x + (R+\Lambda_1) x_{t-1} - R\Lambda_1 x_{t-2} + U_1 p_{t-1} + U_2 p_{t-2} + \ldots + U_q p_{t-q}$$
$$+ \xi_t^x \qquad (IV.14)$$

with $c^x = c^x(c^p, \alpha, A, B, R, \tau, \delta)$;

$\Lambda_1 = \Lambda_1(A, B, \tau)$;

$U_j = R\tilde{Q}_{j-1} - \tilde{Q}_0 Q_j - \tilde{Q}_j = U_j(A, B, R, Q_1, \ldots, Q_q, \tau, \delta)$, $j = 1, \ldots, q-1$;

$U_q = R\tilde{Q}_{q-1} - \tilde{Q}_0 Q_q = U_q(A, B, R, Q_1, \ldots, Q_q, \tau, \delta)$;

and $\tilde{\xi}_t^x = (\xi_t^s - \tilde{Q}_0 \xi_t^p)$ being the innovations in factor inputs.

Equation (IV.14) is a closed form solution of (IV.5). The overidentifying restrictions and relationships between the parameters of the structural equations (IV.1), (IV.2), (IV.3), (IV.10) and (IV.12), and the factor demand equations (IV.14) can be made explicit. An important restriction is the diagonality of the adjustment matrix Λ_1 : In a rational expectations model with a quadratic objective function the occurrence of trade-offs of costs (the nondiagonality of matrix B) or of complementarity in the production (the nondiagonality of matrix A) does not lead to interrelatedness in the adjustment process. Interrelated multivariate adjustment, however, results from serial cross-correlation of the unforeseen shocks in the firms technology (the nondiagonality of matrix R).

A second important finding is that the stability of the autoregressive part of equation (IV.14) follows from the proper-ties of Λ_1 and R. In this model a non-stationarity in x_t results from non-stationary factor prices.

The explicitness of the closed from solution (IV.14) enables us to identify the impact of a change in the process for exogenous prices on the firm's factor demand. For instance, a (structural) step change in the real price level, c^p, which is immediately recognized as such, will lead to a step change in factor demand, c^x. The magnitude of the step change in factor demand, however, depends also on the size of adjustment costs (B) and the firm's technology (α,A).

A structural change in the autoregressive part of the process for real input prices, $Q_1, \ldots, Q_q$, influences the factor input decisions through price effects U_i. However, the agent may not immediately correctly assess size and sign of a change in the parameters of Q_i, in which case the firm's uncertainty about the environment is increased. As a result the (subjective) variances of the innovations increase. When more information about the exogenous variables becomes available, the uncertainty about the structure of the process of the exogenous variables will decrease again.

Consequently, the process of learning about the nature and size of the structural change in Q_i may possibly induce autoregressive conditional heteroskedasticity (ARCH) in the disturbances of the dynamic factor demand equations (IV.14).

The explicit closed form solution (IV.14) also throws light on the identification problem of the structural parameters. EY argue that the technological parameters $(\alpha, \delta, \tau, A, B)$ and the parameters of the exogenous variables $(R, Q_1, \ldots, Q_q)$ can only be identified if the output supply equation is included in the system to be estimated. We find that under RE's this is only true for the off-diagonal parameters of A and B, the real discount rate τ, and the capital depreciation rate δ.

Finally, innovations in technology and prices lead to innova-

tions in demand, since $\xi^x_t = \xi^s_t - \tilde{Q}_0 \xi^p_t$. Accordingly, the disturbances of (IV.12) and (IV.14), $\xi_t = (\xi^{p'}_t, \xi^{x'}_t)'$, are contemporaneously correlated. In the sequel we assume that ξ_t is independently normally distributed with zero mean and an unrestricted
symmetric positive definite covariance matrix Σ.

4.3 An Empirical Analysis

In this section, we apply the model (IV.12) and (IV.14) to quarterly aggre gate manufacturing data in the Netherlands for the
period 1971.I-1984.IV.   In figure 1 time series are given for
aggregate employment (ℓ), capital (k), real labour costs (w) and
real prices of investments (q), the base year for all data being
1980.   A description of the data sources is given   in appendix
A.5.   In the empirical analysis n equals 1.
Unfortunately time series on branches of industry are not
available for the Netherlands.   Therefore we have to rely on
sectoral aggregates.   We cannot take into account the shifts
within the industry.   In the last two decades some branches of
the industry threatened to collapse under the increasing production costs and the growing foreign competition (e.g. textile,
paper, shipbuilding), whereas capital and know-how-intensive
industries, such as chemistry and electrotechnology, experienced
a substantial expansion.

Energy supply and prices were strongly affected by the world oil crises which occurred in 1973.IV (OC1) and in 1979.II (OC2). OC1 reduced the profitability of firms. Heavy foreign competition prohibited the price increases necessary to cover the increase of production costs. Sales fell off as a result of depressed demand. Bankruptcy was a major cause of rising unemployment.

Anticipating price increases due to OC2 the export of energy intensive industries such as chemistry and steel expanded. In our analysis, however, we do not discuss the effects of a foreseen price change, but the impact of OC2 on wage costs and factor demand after it had occured.

The slow-down of the growth of domestic sales was caused by the decrease of real disposable income. The market share of imported goods increased again. Employment decreased and profit shares deteriorated in the years after OC2. Wage restraints reduced the ratio of wage costs to total production costs (see figure IV.1).

We start our empirical investigation with an analysis of the single data series. First, we test for the order of integration of the series. We assume that each time series can be adequately represented by the univariate model

$$\hat{v}_t - v_{t-1} = \beta_0 + \beta_1 OC_1 + \beta_2 OC_2 + \alpha_1 v_{t-1} + \alpha_2 \Delta v_{t-1} + \epsilon_t, \quad (IV.1.1)$$

where OC_1 and OC_2 are oil shock dummies being 1 for 1973.IV and 1979.II respectively and zero otherwise, if the model is estimated in first differences, and being 1 for the periods 1973.IV-1984.IV and 1979.II-1984.IV respectively and zero otherwise if the model is estimated in levels; ϵ_t is an i.i.d. $N(0,\sigma^2)$ random variable; and $V_t \in \{w_t, q_t, \ell_t, k_t\}$. Three dummies were added to the equation to account for seasonality in the data.

To test the hypothesis that the second order process V_t has a unit root without a drift, or $H_0 : \alpha_1 = 0$, we computed Fuller's $\hat{\tau}_\tau$ yielding -1.38, -1.99, $-.79$ and $-.15$ for w_t, q_t, ℓ_t and k_t respectively, with $\bar{R}^2$ being .987, .897, .997 and .998, and the DW being 2.05, 1.95, 2.08 and 2.01 respectively. Consequently, on the basis of a comparison with the values in table 8.5.2. of Fuller (1976) we cannot reject the hypotheses of w_t, q_t, ℓ_t and k_t being I(1).

In the RE-model (IV.14) the autoregressive part of ℓ_t and k_t is restricted to be stationary. Yet, figure IV.1 clearly indicates that both series are non-stationary. In the literature, a non-stationarity is often viewed as being beyond the scope of the economic model, and is remedied by incorporating deterministic trends. However, when factor demand and real input prices are cointegrated, the non-stationarity of the latter may capture that of the input demand. To test for cointegration we compute

the cointegrating regressions for ℓ_t and k_t and the correspon-

ding augmented Dickey-Fuller regressions for the period

1971.I-1984.IV, and find (asymptotic t-statistics are given

within parentheses, seasonal dummies are reported).

Figure IV.1 : Factor Inputs and Real Input Prices of the Dutch

Manufacturing Sector (1971.I - 1984.IV).

Index numbers manufacturing employment
(1980=100)

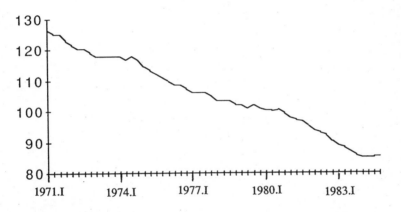

Real price index manufacturing labour costs
(1980=1   )

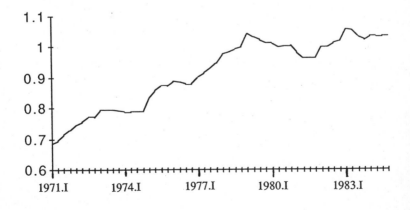

Figure IV.1 : Factor Inputs and Real Input Prices of the Dutch
Manufacturing Sector (1971.I - 1984.IV).

Index numbers capital stock (1980=100)

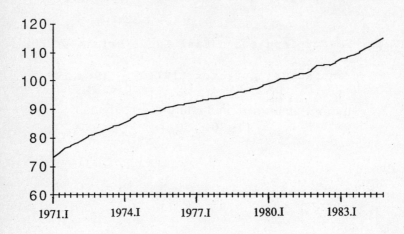

Real price index capital stock
(1980=1   )

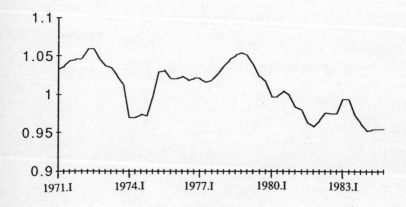

$$\hat{\ell}_t = .464 + .085 \; OC_1 + .034 \; OC_2 - 1.164 \; w_t + 1.563 \; q_t \quad (+ \; u_t^\ell)$$

$$(2.85) \quad (4.77) \qquad (2.21) \qquad (-15.35) \qquad (8.76) \qquad\qquad (IV.2.1)$$

$$\bar{R}^2 = .964; \; DW = .620$$

$$\hat{\Delta u}_t^\ell = -.317 \; u_{t-1}^\ell - .001 \; \Delta u_{t-1}^\ell \qquad\qquad (IV.2.2)$$

$$(-3.14) \qquad (-.22)$$

$$\hat{k}_t = 1.740 - .047 \; OC_1 - .029 \; OC_2 + .917 \; w_t - 1.580 \; q_t \quad (+ \; u_t^k)$$

$$(14.21) \quad (-3.91) \qquad (-2.69) \qquad (17.22) \qquad (-11.70) \qquad (IV.2.3)$$

$$\bar{R}^2 = .976; \; DW = .774$$

$$\hat{\Delta u}_t^k = -.375 \; u_{t-1}^k - .001 \; \Delta u_{t-1}^k \; . \qquad\qquad (IV.2.4)$$

$$(-3.29) \qquad (-.93)$$

The CRDW-statistics (Cointegrating Regressions Durbin-Watson statistic) are .620 and .774 for ℓ_t and k_t respectively. By comparison of higher order cointegrated systems of Engle and Yoo (1987), the CRDW-statistics seem to reject the null at a 5 percent level, indicating that both ℓ_t and k_t are cointegrated with factor prices. A similar conclusion can be drawn from the augmented Dickey-Fuller (ADF)-statistic, with values -3.14 and -3.29 respectively; using tables II and III of Engle and Yoo, the null is rejected at a 10% level for ℓ_t and k_t. Accordingly, ℓ_t and k_t may be viewed as being cointegrated with w_t and q_t. Excluding OC_1 and OC_2 from the cointegrating regressions we find .16 and .35 for the CRDW-statistics of ℓ_t and k_t respectively and −1.33 and −1.57 for the ADF-statistics. This finding and the t-statistics of OC_1 and OC_2 in both cointegrating regressions indicate that ℓ_t and k_t have undergone (structural) step changes due to price increases of OC_1 and OC_2.

Excluding the seasonal dummies from the cointegrating regressions leads to even stronger support for the cointegrating assumption, with CRDW-statistics that equal .757 and 1.057 respectively, and ADF-statistics yielding −3.50 and −4.31. This finding indicates that the long run relationship between the cointegrating variables has been distinctively different for each season.

The cointegrated system must have a causal ordering in at least one direction (Engle and Granger, 1987). In section 2, we assumed unidirectional causal ordering in the sense of Granger from prices to factor demand. We use a fourth order VAR of w_t, q_t, ℓ_t and k_t in levels, including a constant, OC_1 and OC_2, and three seasonal dummies, to test the hypothesis that the coefficients of all lagged factor inputs in the price equations are zero. The size of the WALD test may be smaller than the nominal size because of the possible occurence of unit roots. Consequently, a WALD test, being computed from a regression in levels, that rejects the hypothesis of Granger causality, implicitly rejects the hypothesis when the estimation was carried out in first differences. The WALD statistic which is asymptotically

χ^2 (16) distributed equals 24.38. The WALD statistic associated with the null hypothesis of no causality from prices to demand equals 38.26 and is significantly different from zero at a 1 % level (df = 16). In conclusion we can say that unidirectional causality from input prices to factor demand is found to be in accordance with the information in the data.

Under the null hypothesis of unidirectional causality from input prices to factor demand, we can examine the process for the price series independently from the factor input data. Bivariate identification of $p_t = (w_t, q_t)'$ has been carried out using the SCA statistical system provided by Liu et.al. (1986). The results for Akaike's Information Criterion (AIC) and a statistic, CHI^2, testing the significance of an additional lag of the bivariate lag-polynomial, are given in table IV.1. CHI^2 is based on the logarithmic difference of the residual covariance matrix ML-estimates of autoregressions with and without an additional lag and is asymptotically χ^2 (4) distributed. On the basis of the results in table 1 and the tests for unit roots we assume that the process of p_t can be adequately modeled as follows

$$\Delta p_t = c_0^p + c_1^p \ OC_1 + c_2^p \ OC_2 + Q\Delta p_{t-1} + \xi_t^p, \qquad (IV.3.1)$$

where c_0^p is a (2x4)-matrix including a constant and three seasonal dummies, c_1^p and c_2^p are 2-vectors and Q is a (2×2)-matrix of constant parameters.

Table IV.1 : Bivariate order selection of p = (w,q)'.

	p_{-1}	p_{-2}	p_{-3}	p_{-4}
CHI^2	93.67	20.57	.90	5.18
AIC	-15.75	-16.12	-16.00	-15.99

	Δp_{-1}	Δp_{-2}	Δp_{-3}	Δp_{-4}
CHI^2	25.94	2.57	4.52	5.65
AIC	-16.01	-15.94	-15.91	-15.93

Basically, x_t can be written as the partial adjustment model (IV.9). Moreover x_t and p_t were found to be I(1). In that case it can be shown (cf. Nickell (1985)) that equation (IV.9) will reduce to an error correction mechanism (see appendix A.3). According to the Granger Representation Theorem (see Engle and Granger (1987)) and the results of (IV.2.1)-(IV.2.4) this implies that the theoretical considerations indicate that x_t and p_t should cointegrate. This finding has been confirmed empirically.

For reasons explained in the previous section we assume that the structural parameter matrices A and B are diagonal, without loss of generality. Then the dynamic factor input demand equation (IV.14) becomes

$$x_t = c^x_0 + c^x_1 OC_1 + c^x_2 OC_2 + (R+\Lambda_1)x_{t-1} - R\Lambda_1 x_{t-2} + U_1 p_{t-1} +$$

$$+ U_2 p_{t-2} + \xi^x_t, \qquad\qquad\qquad\qquad (IV.4.1)$$

where $U_1 = (I-R)\Lambda_1 B^{-1}V + (I+d-\tau\Lambda_1)\Lambda_1 B^{-1}VQ,$

$U_2 = (I-R)(d-\tau\Lambda_1)\Lambda_1 B^{-1}VQ,$

V is a (2×2)-matrix solving $\tau\Lambda_1 V(I+Q)-(\tau\Lambda_1)^2 VQ = I,$

and ξ^x_t is a 2-vector of innovations.

Note that $C^{-1} \Lambda^i_1 C = \Lambda^i_1$, since $C = I$ if A and B are diagonal. The 4-vector of disturbances $(\xi^p_t{'},\xi^x_t{'})'$ is assumed to be i.i.d. $N(0,\Sigma)$ distributed.

Seasonal dummies were added to the regression equations to take account of the seasonality in the data.

Estimates of the structural parameters of the system (IV.3.1) and (IV.4.1) are obtained using the method of asymptotic least squares (ALS).

The nonlinear functions are known when a closed form solution has been obtained, as described in section 2. The ALS-estimation results are given in table IV.2. On a priori grounds we assume the quarterly real discount factor τ to be .98; the depreciation rate δ for capital is set equal to .047, for the period 1971-1984 and has been obtained from the CBS.

The assumptions underlying our model appear to be corroborated.

The technological shocks follow a stationary process, and the structural matrices A and B are positive definite. The adjustment costs of labor are smaller than those of capital ($B_{11} < B_{22}$), and B_{11} is not significantly different from zero. This finding is intuitively plausible, and is consistent with findings from similar comparable empirical research (see e.g. Pindyck and Rotemberg (1983)).

Apart from the likelihood ratio (LR)-statistic, testing the appropriateness of the parameter restrictions implied by the theoretical model and which is significant at the 5 % level but not at the 1 % level, the bottom part of table 2 shows that the model fits the data fairly well. Although the Durbin-Watson statistic is biased towards 2, the values are very close to 2, which is remarkably good for this type of dynamic model. The consistent multivariate portmanteau test statistic of Hosking (1980) is an LM test and does not point to any higher order significant residual autocorrelation. The significance at the 5% level (but not at the 1% level), of the LR-statistic may be due to the rather simple functional form of the firm's technology and costs structure.

The ARCH-statistics in table IV.2 (see Engle (1982)), do not indicate any significant residual autoregressive conditional heteroskedasticity. This finding suggests that the agents' learning in the presence of a structural change has indeed been modeled in a way that is not in contradiction with sample evidence, by adding dummy variables for the effects on demand of a step change in the process of input prices. OC_1 leads to a significant scrapping of capital. OC_2 significantly reduced the demand for labor, thereby increasing the unemployment in the Netherlands.

Table IV.2 : ALS-estimation results and tests of the RE-factor

demand model for the period 1971.III–1984.IV*

$$p = (w,q)' :$$

$$c^p = \begin{bmatrix} .019 & (5.95) \\ -.002 & (.63) \end{bmatrix} \qquad OC_1 = \begin{bmatrix} .001 & (.13) \\ .004 & (.45) \end{bmatrix}$$

$$OC_2 = \begin{bmatrix} -.022 & (1.90) \\ -.018 & (2.24) \end{bmatrix} \qquad Q = \begin{bmatrix} .394 & (2.02) & .146 & (.66) \\ .147 & (.85) & .293 & (1.51) \end{bmatrix}$$

$$x = (\ell,k)' :$$

$$c^x = \begin{bmatrix} .006 & (.34) \\ .005 & (.49) \end{bmatrix} \qquad OC_1 = \begin{bmatrix} .003 & (1.32) \\ -.005 & (2.41) \end{bmatrix}$$

$$OC_2 = \begin{bmatrix} -.007 & (2.06) \\ .001 & (.20) \end{bmatrix} \qquad R = \begin{bmatrix} .886 & (1.58) & .127 & (.97) \\ -.173 & (.189) & .232 & (1.35) \end{bmatrix}$$

* The absolute values of asymptotic t-values are given within
  parentheses. The estimated coefficients of seasonal dummies
  have not been presented in the table.

<u>Table IV.2</u> : ALS-estimation results and tests of the RE-factor

demand model for the period 1971.III-1984.IV *

$$x = (\ell,k)':$$

$$A = \begin{bmatrix} 1.774 \ (.28) & 0 \\ 0 & 1.450 \ (2.20) \end{bmatrix} \quad B = \begin{bmatrix} .354 \ (.39) & 0 \\ 0 & .730 \ (4.62) \end{bmatrix}$$

$$\Sigma_4 = \begin{bmatrix} 12.23 & & & \\ 7.65 & 9.88 & & \\ -1.20 & -2.21 & 2.82 & \\ -.24 & .33 & .21 & 1.21 \end{bmatrix} \times 10^{-5} \quad \log L = 795.55$$

TESTS :   Hosking : $\chi^2(16s-12)$ ARCH : $\chi^2(s)$

	s	LM	$\chi^2(.95)$	s	w	q	ℓ	k
DW(w) = 1.99	5	68.25	88.25	1	.35	.09	.24	.01
DW(q) = 1.84	10	144.62	177.39	2	.94	.11	2.33	2.87
DW(ℓ) = 1.91	15	226.28	264.23	3	1.99	.55	2.49	5.65
DW(k) = 2.10	20	300.68	349.93	4	3.40	5.70	2.99	5.56
LR(8) = 19.94								

* The absolute values of asymptotic t-values are given within parentheses. The estimated coefficients of seasonal dummies have not been presented in the table.

4.4 Concluding Remarks

This chapter has been concerned with the multivariate adjustment rational expectations model. A solution of the stochastic control problem of the firm has been given and the implications of the theoretical model for the factor demand equations have been discussed. In particular, it has been shown that interrelation between factor demand does not result from possibilities for substitution between inputs or trade-off in the adjustment costs. It can result from the cross-correlation between the shocks affecting the production technology of the firm. In line with the Lucas critique, special attention was paid to the implications of a structural change in the processes generating the exogenous variables. Finally, the model has been applied to quarterly data for the manufacturing in the Netherlands for the period 1971-1984.

As the hypothesis of cointegration of factor demand series and relative factor prices was not rejected by the data, the nonstationarity of the factor demand series has been modeled by including the levels of the relative prices in the demand schedules, instead of detrending them prior to the analysis.

To summarize, the following conclusions were reached.

(i)   A quadratic objective function does not imply interrelated adjustments of production factors. Cross-correlation of innovations in the production technology, however, does.

(ii)   In line with the RE hypothesis, the nonstationarity of the factor demand series can be accounted for by the nonstationarity in the exogenous variables.

(iii)   A structural step change in the constant term of the process of the exogenous variables leads to a step change in the factor demand equations. The magnitude of the change depends on the size of adjustment costs and the firm's technology.

(iv)   The gradual learning about the nature of the structural change may induce patterns in the disturbances of the demand system that can be approximated by an ARCH-process.

(v)   For the Dutch manufacturing sector, labor and capital and their prices relative to the output price index are integrated of order one. Moreover, the four series are found to be cointegrated.

In order to prevent a misinterpretation of these results, some qualifications have to be made. First, the empirical analysis was based on aggregate data. Aggregation possibly hides the differences in the adjustments that have taken place in the various branches of the industry. Second, the rejection of the restrictions implied by the RE-adjustment cost model at the 5 % level may be the result of the rather simple functional form of the production function and of the adjustment cost structure, a criticism which has often been made in the literature (e.g. Morrison (1986)). More complicated functional forms lead to nonlinear first order conditions for the optimization problem and may be prohibitive for getting a closed form solution in which case the Euler equations can be analyzed using for instance an instrumental variables technique (e.g. Hansen and Singleton (1982)).

CHAPTER 5 : THE STRUCTURE OF ADJUSTMENT COSTS FOR LABOUR IN THE DUTCH MANUFACTURING SECTOR

5.1 Introduction

This chapter examines the appropriateness of symmetric quadratic specifications of adjustment costs for labour (ACL) in dynamic labour demand models. We interviewed personnel managers of Dutch manufacturing firms. The interviews focussed on decisions of firms to change their productive workforce and the costs that arise from these changes. The general outcomes of the interviews are discussed in section 2.

In section 3 we propose an alternative ACL specification which satisfies the properties of the dynamic theory of labour demand and includes the symmetric quadratic form as a special case.

The merit of the novel specification is the possibility to measure the difference between hiring costs and firing costs. Econometric analysis of the alternative ACL function using data obtained from annual reports of Dutch manufacturing firms for the period 1978-1986 show that hiring costs exceed firing costs. This finding has an important implication. The speed of adjustment of the firm's workforce to a moving target level is slower in economic uprises than it is in economic recessions. Conclusions are drawn in section 4.

5.2 ACL in Practice

In order to get a better insight into the structure of ACL in practice we interviewed personnel managers of DSM chemicals, FOKKER aircrafts, HOOGOVENS steel, VENDEX International and VOLVO cars. The interviews focussed on decisions of the firms to change their productive workforce and the costs that arise from these changes. The choice of firms has been such that together they represent the Dutch manufacturing sector as a whole. The firms are relatively large with outlets that reach beyond domestic markets. The various firms reflect differences in production technologies, that is, differences in production processes, required technological knowledge, and the input of labour as a production factor. In this section we present the most salient outcomes of the interviews.

FOKKER and HOOGOVENS stated that the rate of labour turnover amounts to 5 percent of the total workforce per six months. Although start up costs of new entries are inversely related to the capacity and quality of a firm's training department, the turnover adjustment costs of labour do not increase at the margin. However, a growth up to 5 percent yield marginally increasing ACL, whereas an increase over 5 percent is practically impossible, since this will lead to large inefficiencies in the production process. If these statements hold true in general, the ACL function should be adjusted for the size of the firm.

The personnel managers of all the firms agreed that ACL depend on union power, the expectation formation of labour input requirements in the near future and production technology. Labour unions have a considerable effect on the costs of labour adjustments through their influence on the rate of dismissal payments and the duration of application terms for dismissals. Tight dismissal regulations and high dismissal payments boost ACL. Given the power of labour unions, a firm that accurately forecasts its future sales and, accordingly, its future labour input minimizes ACL when the firm changes its workforce. The longer it takes firms to fire their workers, the higher are ACL when employment expectations do not match future realizations. A dismissal application lasts between six and twelve months.

Consequently, a firm that wants to reduce the workforce below
the level of its labour turnover rate must start the dismissal
procedure this period in advance. Figure 1a and 1b[1] illustrate
how a firm's expectation formation process of labour input
requirements in the near future reduces ACL. We assume that a
firm is confronted with an unforeseen structural change in its
economic environment at t=1, such that a decrease in employment
becomes necessary. Given that the dismissal application term
lasts one period, and assuming that the firm gradually reduces
the workforce over one period, the costs of inefficient
employment policy equals the labour surplus (shaded areas) times
the average wage costs of these workers. In figure 1a the firm's
expectation formation process is rational, that is, it takes
account of the tight dismissal regulations and applies for the
firing of $L_1^e - L_3^e$ workers at time t=1. Figure 1b shows the ACL of
a firm with myopic foresight, which takes employment decisions
structurally one period too late. At t=1 it applies for the
dismissal of $L_2^e - L_1$, at t=2 it applies for the dismissal of
$L_3^e - L_2$, and so on. During the time that the firm's target level
of employment (L^e) does not remain constant the firm has a
structural labour surplus.

----

1) These figures were initially drawn by Ir. J. Zaaier of
   FOKKER.

Consequently, we may conclude that the expectations formation process of the firm is of crucial importance as to minimize the adjustment costs of labour. In a changing economic environment forces that limit the firms to adjust optimally to these changes, such as long application terms for dismissals, boost ACL.

The extend to which ACL influence the firm's reaction to a changing economic environment depends also on the labour-intensity of the production process. Firms with a high-tech labour-intensive production process, such as aircraft industries (FOKKER), face high costs of labour adjustments. These firms employ relatively many highly qualified workers, with large hiring and training costs. ACL differ significantly between skilled and unskilled workers. This fact, surveyed in Nickell (1986), has also been underlined by the personnel managers of the Dutch firms. ACL of unskilled workers are low in comparison with their variable wage costs. Firms using low-level know-how labour-intensive production technologies employ mainly unskilled recruits. For these firms variation in workforce is an important instrument to change output and production costs. Figure 2 illustrates employment reductions when production costs rise above a permissable level and the board of directors cuts these costs through reducing the workforce [1]. Given that the firm's

----

[1] Figure 2 was initially drawn by B. van Dijk of VOLVO Cars. He called it "indentation employment policy".

Figure 1a : ACL caused by once-only expectational error in a case
of tight dismissal regulations.

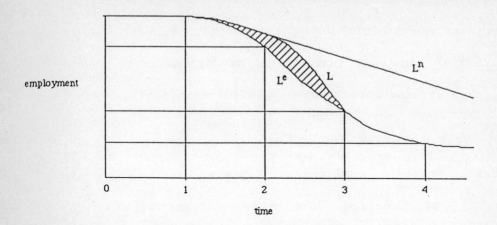

Figure 1b : ACL caused by a structural expectation error of one period
in the case of tight dismissal regulations.

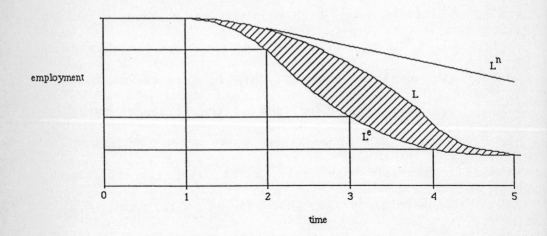

L_t = the number of workers employed at period t

L_t^e = the firm's target level of employment at period t

L_t^n = the firm's workforce at period t reduced only by labour turnover

departments are inclined to grow in size, with low ACL and in the absence of dismissal regulations, the least productive and relatively most expensive workers are fired at t=1, t=2, etc.

In spite of the fact that ACL are low, this model leads to a cyclical pattern in the dynamic demand of labour.

Decisions to change the production capacity of a capital-intensive firm, such as steel (HOOGOVENS) and chemical industries (DSM), are not based on considerations of personnel costs. Such firms develop a marketing plan, which is followed by an investment plan, from which the employment plan is derived. Investment decisions are based on the product market, that is, the expectations of future product demand. The time lag between the investment decision and the resulting demand for labour equals two years on average. Costs of recruiting, screening and training are less than one percent of the total investment. The ACL are part of the investment and are written down as such together with the new capital.

5.3 The Shape of the ACL Function

In this section we discuss the shape of the function that relates costs to the rate of workforce adjustments. Nickell (1986) discusses several likely forms of ACL functions and their implications for dynamic labour demand theory. The linear adjustment cost model, for instance, is found to be consistent with the

<u>Figure 2</u> : Indentation employment policy.

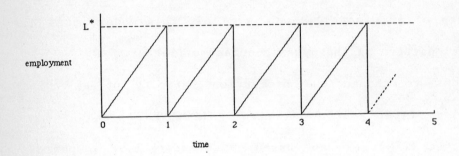

instantaneous hiring and firing of groups of workers. In the linear model there is no partial adjustment to the new long-run equilibrium, and consequently labour demand is not dynamic.

As has been pointed out by Oi (1962), however, when labour is a quasi-fixed production factor, labour demand follows an autoregressive process. In the dynamic theory of the firm it is assumed that ACL is represented by a strictly convex function with the following properties (n=number of workers employed, Δn= change in employment in one period).

P_1: $ACL(\Delta n) \ |_{\Delta n=0} = 0$;

P_2: $\partial ACL(\Delta n)/\partial n \ \substack{>\\<} \ 0$, if $\Delta n \ \substack{>\\<} \ 0$;

P_3: $\partial^2 ACL(\Delta n)/\partial n^2 > 0$.

The symmetric quadratic function which satisfies these properties is as follows.

$$ACL (\Delta n) = \gamma(\Delta n)^2 \qquad \gamma > 0. \qquad (V.1)$$

In this section we propose an alternative ACL function which
measures the asymmetry between hiring and firing costs. The
novel specification encompasses the quadratic form as a special
case. The function is as follows

$$ACL (\Delta n) = \alpha - \beta\Delta n + \gamma(\Delta n)^2 + \exp(\delta\Delta n) - 1, \qquad (V.2)$$

where α, β, γ and δ are constant parameters. P_1 to P_3 are
satisfied in the following restricted version of (V.2).

$$ACL (\Delta n) = -\beta\Delta n + \gamma(\Delta n)^2 + \exp(\beta\Delta n) - 1, \qquad (V.3)$$

where $\alpha=0$ and $\beta=\delta$. ACL represented by equation (V.3) is not symmetric in case of $\beta\neq0$. If $\beta > 0$ hiring costs are marginally
higher than firing costs. If $\beta < 0$ firing costs exceed hiring
costs (see figure V.3).

In order to estimate the ACL function we collected data on net
changes in workforce per year and the corresponding ACL from
annual reports of Dutch manufacturing firms for the period
1978-1986. Annual reports do not specify ACL but some of them
contain the entry "total costs of reorganisation", which we
assume to be a proxy for ACL. ACL are measured in thousands of

guilders and have been deflated by the 1980 = 100 producers price index of domestic sales. Net changes in employment (Δn) are expressed in hundreds of workers. The sample consists of 168 cases (9 years and 30 firms and 102 missing observations). For 119 cases firings exceeded hirings ($\Delta n < 0$), whereas the workforce increased in 49 cases ($\Delta n > 0$). This corresponds to the overall employment trends in the Netherlands over the spell.

We regressed the data on several forms of the ACL function. This allows us to test the importance of fixed costs ($\alpha \neq 0$). We note that ACL is measured as total costs instead of variable costs. An example of fixed ACL is the fact that training departments are expensive even if no newly hired workers are trained. The estimation of the flexible form (V.2) also allows us to test the validity of the restrictions on the parameters implied by the dynamic theory (V.3) or the restrictions implied by the symmetric quadratic shape of ACL (V.1). Results are given in table V.1.

Chow's test on parameter stability (F_1) between the periods 1978-1982 and 1983-1986 does not point at any structural change in the parameters through time. This justifies regarding the data as a panel, and assuming the parameters of relation (V.2) to be time-independent. The F_2-statistic tests the hypothesis

Figure 3 : The structure of ACL represented by equation V.3.

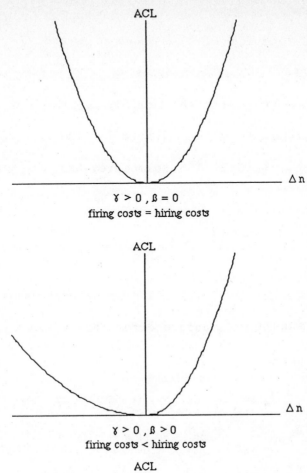

ACL

$\gamma > 0$, $\beta = 0$
firing costs = hiring costs

ACL

$\gamma > 0$, $\beta > 0$
firing costs < hiring costs

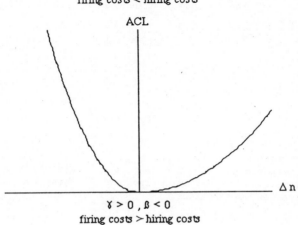

ACL

$\gamma > 0$, $\beta < 0$
firing costs > hiring costs

that the parameters in (V.2) do not change with the size of the firm. The sample has been devided into 91 cases of firms with less than 5000 employees on the one hand and 77 cases of firms that have 5000 or more employees on the other hand. The statistic F_2 does not reject the hypothesis, which implies that the ACL function should not be adjusted by the size of the firm, as suggested in section 2. The Kolmogarov-Smirnov test (KS) point at some deviation from normality of the residuals, which implies that the tests may be biased.

Table V.1 : Estimation Results and Hypothesis Tests of the ACL Function (standard errors are given within parentheses).

	α	β	γ	δ	$\bar{R}^2$	χ^2
1: Unrestricted [equation (V.2)]	α=4.45 (1.50)	β=1.02 (.17)	γ=-.11 E-2 (.13 E-2)	δ=.22 (.03)	$\bar{R}^2$=.59	
2: $\beta=\delta$	α=6.64 (1.54)	β=.20 (.05)	γ=.51 E-2 (.06 E-2)	δ=.20 (.05)	$\bar{R}^2$=.52	$\chi^2(1)$=25.62
3: $\beta=\delta=0$	α=7.43 (1.52)	--	γ=.66 E-2 (.05 E-2)	--	$\bar{R}^2$=.50	$\chi^2(2)$=25.82
4: $\alpha=0$; $\beta=\delta$ [equation (V.3)]	--	β=.23 (.03)	γ=.54 E-2 (.06 E-2)	δ=.23 (.03)	$\bar{R}^2$=.47	$\chi^2(2)$=47.73
5: $\alpha=\beta=\delta=0$ [equation (V.1)]	--	--	γ=.71 E-2 (.05 E-2)	--	$\bar{R}^2$=.43	$\chi^2(3)$=102.32

Tests : Normality   : KS = 3.38
         Parameter constancy through time   : $F_1(4,160)$ = 1.92
         Parameter constancy over firm size   : $F_2(4,160)$ = 1.33
         Number of Observations   : 168

Wald's tests (χ^2) on parameter restrictions and the adjusted $\bar{R}^2$ given in table V.1 show that the flexible ACL function (3.2) is superior to all the alternatives, including the symmetric quadratic form with a constant term measuring fixed ACL (specification 3, table V.1) and equation (V.1) (specification 5, table V.1). Besides, the parameter restrictions implied by P_1 to P_3 are not in accordance with the data. Moreover, the parameter estimates indicate that ACL are basically not symmetric. The estimates of β and δ being both significantly greater than zero indicate that hiring costs exceed firing costs in the period 1978-1986. This finding has an important implication. The speed of employment adjustment to a (higher) target level of expanding firms is slower than the speed of employment adjustment to a (lower) target level of shrinking firms. Or, stated differently, during economic booms (hirings exceeding firings) employment will be lagged more behind the target level than during recessions (firings exceeding hirings).

5.4 Conclusions

From interviews we have had with personnel managers of a selection of Dutch manufacturing firms we found that the costs of labour adjustments to a new target level depend on the expectations formation process of a firm, and the labour-intensity of a firm's production process. Labour unions have a substantial effect on ACL through the bargained rate of dismissal payments and the duration of dismissal application terms. This finding is in accordance with recent research in the UK (Burgess, 1988, Burgess and Dolado, 1988).

Next, we have presented an alternative ACL function that measures the asymmetry between hiring and firing costs, and encompasses the symmetric quadratic form commonly used in models of dynamic labour demand as a special case. Under certain restrictions the novel specification of ACL, satisfies the properties of the dynamic theory of the firm. Estimation of the ACL function showed that in the period 1978-1986 hiring costs exceed firing costs in the Dutch manufacturing sector. Accordingly, during economic booms, a firm's employment will be more lagged behind its target level than during periods of recession. We also found that ACL consist of both variable costs, as well as fixed costs that do not vary with the size of the adjustment. Results in support of this conclusion are given by recent research on the structure of adjustment costs for labour faced by US manufacturing firms (Hamermesh, 1988).

Implementation of the ACL function into dynamic factor demand models and empirical examination of the differences in hiring and firing costs between production and non-production workers in manufacturing firms will be presented in the next chapter.

CHAPTER 6 : ASYMMETRIC ADJUSTMENT COSTS OF LABOUR IN NONLINEAR RATIONAL EXPECTATIONS DEMAND MODELS

6.1 Introduction

The costs of hiring a worker generally differ in size from the firing costs. This chapter investigates the implications of asymmetric costs for production and nonproduction workers. It makes three contributions. First, two rational expectations asymmetric adjustment cost models of the firm are analysed. In one model, capital is assumed to be predetermined when employment decisions are taken. The other assumes that investment and employment decisions are taken simultaneously. Second, the impact of unanticipated shocks in real factor prices, productivity and technology on factor demand is investigated. Third, generalised method of moments (GMM) estimates of the structural parameters of nonlinear optimality conditions for production workers, nonproduction workers and capital, and specification and structural stability tests are presented.

The outline of chapter 6 is as follows. A multivariate labour demand model in which adjustment costs are asymmetric and capital is predetermined is presented in section 2. The impact of a structural break in the process of the forcing variables on the decision rules of the firm is discussed. In section 3 we empirically analyse this model using annual UK manufacturing

109

data for the period 1955 to 1986 and quarterly Dutch manufacturing data for the period 1971.I to 1984.IV.

We find that for both countries, production and nonproduction employment in manufacturing can be adequately explained by means of the long run development of production and nonproduction real wage costs and the capital stock, provided that step changes in the equilibrium levels due to the oil crises are properly taken into account. We also find significant evidence for the asymmetry of adjustment costs. For both the UK and the Netherlands, firing costs of production workers exceed hiring costs, whereas for nonproduction workers hiring seems to be more costly than firing.

In section 4 the model is extended. Capital and employment are simultaneously determined in the model. We present an alternative explanation for the "gestation" lag of the firm's capital as mentioned by Kydland and Prescott (1982) and Rossi (1987) in the form of an asymmetric adjustment cost specification. The forcing variables of the model now become real production and nonproduction wage costs and the real price of capital assets. The analysis of the data casts some doubts upon the stability of the long run relationship between factor inputs and real factor prices. However, the nonstationarity of the decision variables can be adequately explained by simultaneously allowing for common stochastic trends (real input prices) and deterministic trends (technological changes). The asymmetry in adjustment costs of capital appears to be similar in UK and Dutch manufacturing. According to the model, it is optimal for the firm to slow down the scrapping of capital during recessions and to invest during economic uprises in anticipation of higher profits. Finally, conclusions are drawn in section 5.

6.2 Labour Demand under Asymmetric Adjustment Costs and Predetermined Capital

Consider a representative firm which maximizes the expected present value of profits over an infinite horizon with respect to employment assuming that the labour market is competitive. Each decision period the firm chooses an employment contingency plan for n types of labour N_i, $i=1,\ldots,n$, conditional on a predetermined stock of capital and currently available information. Marginal productivity (MP) of labour i at time t is

$$MP(N_{it}) = \alpha_i - \sum_{j=1}^{n} \lambda_{ij} N_{jt} - \kappa_i K_t + \xi_{it}, \quad i=1,\ldots,n, \qquad (VI.1)$$

where α_i, λ_{ij} and κ_i are constant parameters, K_t denotes the firm's capital stock at time t, and ξ_{it} denotes the impact of stochastic technological shocks.

In existing dynamic labour demand models, adjustment costs (AC) are a function of the changes in employment at time t,

$AC(\Delta N_t = (\Delta N_{1t}, \ldots, \Delta N_{nt}))$, such that $\partial AC(\Delta N_t)/\partial N_{it} \gtrless 0$, if

$\Delta N_{it} \gtrless 0$, $\partial AC(\Delta N_t)/\partial N_{it} = AC(0) = 0$ and AC has a positive defi-

nite Hessian matrix. These requirements have traditionally been

implemented by assuming adjustment costs to be a quadratic sym-

metric function of the changes in employment. Symmetry is, of

course, a restrictive assumption as it implies that the costs of

an expansion of the workforce are equal to those of a reduction

of employment.

In chapter five we proposed a more general functional form,

which measures the difference between hiring costs and firing

costs. The quadratric shape is nested in the extended specifi-

cation, whereas it satisfies the convexity conditions of dynamic

theory as well. The specification for the adjustment costs is

as follows

$$AC(\Delta N_{it}) = -\beta_i \Delta N_{it} + \exp(\beta_i \Delta N_{it}) + \tfrac{1}{2} \sum_{j=1}^{n} \gamma_{ij}(\Delta N_{jt})^2, \quad i=1,\ldots,n,$$

$$(VI.2)$$

where γ_{ij} and β_i are constant parameters. Strict convexity is

satisfied iff the Hessian (n×n)-matrix $\partial^2 AC(\Delta N_{it})/\partial^2 N_{jt}$ is posi-

tive definite. If $\beta_i = 0$, equation (VI.2) yields the tradi-

tional quadratic function, being symmetric iff $\gamma_{ij} = \gamma_{ji}$.

What are the implications of asymmetric adjustment costs ? The

long run equilibrium level of employment is not affected since

adjustment costs are assumed to only depend on changes in

employment. But asymmetry has implications for the speed of adjustment to a new equilibrium level.

Assume that the (n×n)-matrix $\Gamma = (\gamma_{ij})$ is positive definite (this is basically assumed in all linear models). If β_i is negative, firing costs of labour i exceed hiring costs and a downward adjustment of employment as a result of a change in the target will take more time than an upward adjustment of employment due to a change in the target of the same size but in opposite direction. Of course, if $\beta_i = 0$ the adjustment pattern will be symmetric.

The objective of the firm is to maximize the real present value of expected profits over an infinite time horizon, given all currently available information. With real wage costs, W_{it}, i=1,...,n, being independent of L_{it} at each period t, the firm chooses employment contingency plans satisfying the following first order (Euler) conditions

$$MP(N_{it}) - MAC(\Delta N_{it}) - W_{it} + \tau\ E[MAC(\Delta N_{it+1})|\Omega_t] = 0, \quad i=1,\ldots,n,$$

$$(VI.3)$$

where MAC is the marginal adjustment cost, τ is a real discount rate and Ω_t is the information set available to the firm at time t.

Together with the transversality conditions, equations (VI.3) define the firm's employment policy. However, current decisions are based on unobserved future expectations. Ideally, one would like to obtain an explicit closed form forward looking solution for (VI.3). For linear first order conditions a closed form solution can be obtained (see e.g. Hansen and Sargent (1981), Kollintzas (1985)), whereas for nonlinear Euler equations this is only occasionally the case.

Explicit forward looking closed form solutions are useful to trace the effects of a structural change in the process generating the forcing variables in the model. In the asymmetric model, however, additional assumptions are needed on the distribution of forecast errors in order to identify the impact of an unanticipated structural change in the exogenous variables. In appendix A.4 we show that the expectational error of a decision variable defined as the difference between the first order condition (VI.3) and that same condition with the expected MAC replaced by the actual MAC is white noise provided the innovation of L_{it+1} is normally distributed. Moreover, an unanticipated shock causing a step change in L_t yields a step change in both unconditional mean and variance of the expectational error of the firm. We also show that an unexpected exogenous shock that leads to a persistent change of the firm's forecast error variance without affecting the slope coefficient of employment (e.g. an increase in uncertainty about the future behaviour of forcing variables) yields a step change in unconditional mean and variance of the firm's expectational error.

Consequently, an unexpected exogenous shock can be modelled by using dummy variables that account for these step changes. Autoregressive conditional heteroscedasticity due to increased uncertainty in the disturbance can be introduced to model the structural break in the variance.

6.3 Empirical Analysis

In this section we present parameter estimates for the optimality conditions in (VI.3). For the empirical analysis of the model we used seasonally unadjusted quarterly data for manufacturing in the Netherlands for the period 1971.I - 1984.IV, and annual data for the manufacturing in the UK for the period 1955-1986. All prices are normalised by dividing by the output price index. All data have been divided by their sample mean. Definitions and data sources are given in appendix A.5. Differences in the adjustment of production workers (N_{1t}) and nonproduction workers (N_{2t}) are due to differences between hiring costs and firing costs of both types of labour (cf. Nickell (1986)). Structural changes in the forcing variables, production and nonproduction real wage costs, W_{1t}, W_{2t}, respectively, and capital K_t, may induce step changes in the employment level and in its variances (see appendix A.4).

In chapter IV we model the learning in the presence of a structural change by including dummy variables in factor demand

equations of a linear model and in the processes for input prices to account for the oil shocks. In line with those findings
we also use dummy variables in the present empirical analysis.
The stochastic first order conditions (VI.3) do not yield a
complete solution to the maximization problem of the firm.   In
order to estimate the structural parameters of the Euler conditions we apply the generalized method of moments (GMM) proprosed
by Hansen (1982) and Hansen and Singleton (1982). The realised
values of period t+1 are substituted for the unobserved expectations of one period ahead employment in (VI.3) and a vector fo-
cast errors, u_{t+1}, of mean zero is added to the system (VI.3)
yielding

$$
\begin{bmatrix} \delta_{01} \\ \delta_{02} \end{bmatrix} \text{CONST} + \begin{bmatrix} \delta_{11} \\ \delta_{21} \end{bmatrix} \text{OC1} + \begin{bmatrix} \delta_{12} \\ \delta_{22} \end{bmatrix} \text{OC2} - \begin{bmatrix} \kappa_1 \\ \kappa_2 \end{bmatrix} K_t - \begin{bmatrix} 1 & 0 \\ 0 & 1 \end{bmatrix} \begin{bmatrix} w_{1t} \\ w_{2t} \end{bmatrix}
$$

$$
- \begin{bmatrix} \lambda_{11} & \lambda_{12} \\ \lambda_{21} & \lambda_{22} \end{bmatrix} \begin{bmatrix} N_{1t} \\ N_{2t} \end{bmatrix} + \begin{bmatrix} \gamma_{11} & \gamma_{12} \\ \gamma_{21} & \gamma_{22} \end{bmatrix} \begin{bmatrix} \Delta N_{1t} - \tau \Delta N_{1t+1} \\ \Delta N_{2t} - \tau \Delta N_{2t+1} \end{bmatrix}
$$

$$
- \begin{bmatrix} \beta_1(\exp(\beta_1 \Delta N_{1t}) - \tau \exp(\beta_1 \Delta N_{1t+1})) \\ \beta_2(\exp(\beta_2 \Delta N_{2t}) - \tau \exp(\beta_2 \Delta N_{2t+1})) \end{bmatrix} = \begin{bmatrix} u_{1t+1} - \xi_{1t} \\ u_{2t+1} - \xi_{2t} \end{bmatrix}, \qquad (VI.4)
$$

where the constant parameters δ_{ij} have replaced the productivity
parameters α_1 and α_2 that are not identified due to a breakdown
into a constant effect and oil shocks step changes (OC1 and OC2
respectively).   The composite error term, $u_{t+1} - \xi_t$, arises from

forecast errors and productivity shocks.

Before proceeding with estimation we discuss the identification of the structural parameters. Normalisation with respect to prices results from the fact that variable real wage costs are assumed to be proportional to labour input. Moreover, contrary to linear closed form solutions, the real discount rate τ is identified in the first order conditions. However, in many applications τ is not very well determined from the Euler equations. One reason for this empirical finding is the nonstationarity of the compound error term due to omitted nonstationary forcing variables (cf. Dolado (1987)). We analyse the integrating properties of the variables in the model. Furthermore, to prevent spurious regression, we test for cointegration between the decision and forcing variables.

First, we investigate the dynamic properties of the univariate series and their order of integration. Table VI.1 presents the results of unit root tests of the production factors N_{1t}, N_{2t} and K_t, and the real factor prices W_{1t}, W_{2t} and Q_t, where Q_t is the real price of capital. According to Fuller's test statistic τ_τ (see Fuller (1976), table 8.5.2) we do not reject the hypothesis that the univariate time series have one unit root.

Second, we test for cointegration between the decision and forcing variables. When these series are cointegrated, the

Table VI.1 : Unit Roots Tests

Model : $\hat{V}_t - V_{t-1} = a'X_t + \alpha_1 V_{t-1} + \alpha_2 \Delta V_{t-1} + \epsilon_t$

$V_t \in \{N_{1t}, N_{2t}, K_t, W_{1t}, W_{2t}, Q_t\}$

$H_0 : \alpha_1 = 0$

The Dutch manufacturing sector : X = (CONST, Q_2, Q_3, Q_4, OC1, OC2)*

$\{V_t : 1971.III - 1984.IV\}$

	N_{1t}	N_{2t}	K_t	W_{1t}	W_{2t}	Q_t
Fuller's $\hat{\tau}_\tau$	-2.48	-.04	-.15	-1.05	-2.16	-1.50
Adjusted R^2	1.00	1.00	1.00	.99	.99	.90
DW-statistic	2.08	2.32	2.01	2.15	2.21	1.95

The UK manufacturing sector : X = (CONST, TREND, OC1, OC2)*

$\{V_t : 1957 - 1986\}$

	N_{1t}	N_{2t}	K_t	W_{1t}	W_{2t}	Q_t
Fuller's $\hat{\tau}_\tau$	-1.96	-.34	-2.00	-.90	-.74	-1.20
Adjusted R^2	.98	.92	1.00	.99	.99	.90
DW-statistic	1.57	2.09	1.50	2.11	1.93	1.95

* Q_2, Q_3 and Q_4 are seasonal dummies, TREND denotes a linear trend, OC1 = 1 in 1973.IV and 1974, OC2 = 1 in 1979.II and 1979 for the Netherlands and the UK respectively and zero otherwise. No linear trend was included for UK capital and the real price of assets.

nonstationarity of N_{1t} and L_{2t} may well be modelled by the nonstationarity of W_{1t}, W_{2t} and K_t. Then equation (VI.4) can be interpreted as an error correction mechanism. Basically, according to the model, the adjustment to a linear long run relationship takes place in a nonlinear way. However, an important property of the concept of stationarity is that it is preserved under some nonlinear transformations (Escribano (1987)).

Consequently, we test for long run equilibrium by computing linear cointegrating regressions. Results are given in table VI.2. Some of the parameters in the long run relationships have "wrong" signs, that is, oil shocks are expected to have had a negative impact on employment, whereas increasing (non)production real wage costs are likely to reduce (non)production employment. The reason for this may be that short term effects overshadow long run relationships, since only a limited number of observations was available for the empirical analysis. Note however, the finding that only nonproduction real wage costs have a significant effect on the employment level of production workers. This finding is consistent for both Dutch and UK manufacturing.

In order to draw inferences we interpolate the critical values of the tables for the Cointegrating Regression Durbin Watson (CRDW) statistics and the Augmented Dickey Fuller (ADF) statistics, applicable to our model.

Comparing the one lag version ADF-statistics given in table VI.2 with the critical values in Engle and Yoo (1987), and comparing the CRDW-statistic with the bounds on critical values given in Sargan and Bhargava (1983), we may draw the following conclusions. The hypothesis of no cointegration is rejected at least at a 5 percent level for Dutch manufacturing nonproduction workers and for both types of employment in UK manufacturing. For manufacturing production workers in the Netherlands, the hypothesis of no cointegration is rejected at a 10 percent level.

If the composite error term in (VI.4) is stationary, τ will be close to unity. Estimating τ turned out to be difficult. No convergence was achieved when τ was estimated. Apparently, this is due to the high nonlinearity in parameters. However, when τ was set equal to unity in the nonlinear expressions of equation (VI.4), the estimate for τ in the linear expressions was .99 with an asymptotic t-value of 22.2 for Dutch data. The UK real discount value was estimated in the same way, resulting in an estimate of .99 with an asymptotic t-value of 17.9. Consequently, τ was set equal to unity prior to estimation.

If the composite error term has a MA(1) representation, instrumental variables have to be used for the future expectations of N_{1t+1} and N_{2t+1} to get consistent estimates. The information sets upon which the GMM estimates are based have been selected by principal component analysis.

Table VI.2 : Cointegration tests : the forcing variables are $\{W_{1t}, W_{2t}, K_t\}$

Cointegrating regressions for the manufacturing sector in the Netherlands[*] (1971.I - 1984.IV)

N_{1t} = 2.33 - .039 OC1 + .025 OC2 - .020 W_{1t} - .252 W_{2t} - 1.03 K_t

   (62.23)   (-4.99)   (3.05)   (-.22)   (-2.57)   (-18.05)

$\bar{R}^2$ = .99   CRDW = .623   ADF = -2.78   T = 56

N_{2t} = 2.13 + .104 OC1 + .014 OC2 - 1.12 W_{1t} + .829 W_{2t} - .937 K_t

   (37.37)   (8.72)   (1.16)   (-7.83)   (5.53)   (-10.70)

$\bar{R}^2$ = .96   CRDW = .965   ADF = -3.91   T = 56

Cointegrating regressions for the manufacturing sector in the UK[*]

1955 - 1986

N_{1t} = 1.29 - .130 OC1 - .048 OC2 + .294 W_{1t} - .893 W_{2t} + .375 K_t

   (31.57)   (-4.83)   (-1.78)   (.91)   (-5.21)   (1.40)

$\bar{R}^2$ = .96   CRDW = 1.01   ADF = -4.91   T = 32

N_{2t} = .430 - .256 OC1 - .020 OC2 + .775 W_{1t} - 1.73 W_{2t} + 1.63 K_t

   (6.46)   (-5.84)   (-.46)   (1.48)   (-6.19)   (3.73)

$\bar{R}^2$ = .82   CRDW = 1.17   ADF = -4.70   T = 32.

[*] Seasonal dummies are not reported. Asymptotic t-values are given within parentheses. OC1 = 1 for the period 1973.IV - 1984.IV and 1974-1986, OC2 = 1 for the period 1979.II - 1984.IV and 1979-1986 for the regressions for the Netherlands and the UK respectively.

For the Netherlands, the instrumental variables (IVs) are two periods lagged production and nonproduction employment, the rate on a three months loan to local authorities, the yield of long term government bonds, and the one period lagged first differences of production and nonproduction real wage costs, real price of capital, capital stock, unemployment rate, and manufacturing output, a constant, three seasonal dummies, OC1 and OC2. The total number of IVs equals 16.

The information set for the UK contains 13 IVs. These are one and two periods lagged production and nonproduction labour and capital, one period lagged first differences of production and nonproduction real wage costs and manufacturing output, one period lagged price of material inputs, a constant, OC1 and OC2.

Table VI.3 contains estimated coefficients and model specification tests. The Sargan-Bhargava statistic (SB) that tests for nonstationarity in the residuals, does not point at a significant random walk behaviour in any of the residual series. Hansen's J-statistic tests overidentifying restrictions of the IV orthogonality conditions. The number of degrees of freedom of the J-test equals the number of structural equations (2) times the number of IVs minus the number of structural parameters in the model (for the Netherlands = 24; UK = 18). The overidentifying restrictions are not rejected at a 5 percent

Table VI.3 : GMM estimation results of structural parameters and tests[*]

Manufacturing sector in the Netherlands[**]
1971.IV - 1984.IV

Production Workers   Nonproduction Workers

δ_{10} : -0.044   (-1.18) δ_{20} : -0.032   (-0.77)
δ_{11} : 0.001   (0.38) δ_{21} : 0.001   (0.83)
δ_{12} : -0.002   (-1.62) δ_{22} : -0.002   (-2.22)
κ_1 : 0.532   (0.49) κ_2 : 0.336   (0.28)
λ_{11} : 0.933   (1.46) λ_{21} : 0.789   (1.10)
λ_{12} : 0.293   (0.78) λ_{22} : 0.176   (0.48)
γ_{11} : 65.768   (2.52) γ_{21} : -1.672   (-0.22)
γ_{12} : -4.955   (-0.79) γ_{22} : 73.819   (1.55)
β_1 : 8.257   (4.45) β_2 : -8.544   (-3.47)

TESTS
SB : 1.77   SB : 2.21

ARCH   ARCH
1   0.13   1   0.13
2   0.38   2   0.20
3   0.88   3   0.54
4   0.77   4   2.16

Overidentifying restrictions   :   5.31 < χ^2 (.95;8)
Symmetric linearity   :   15.42 > χ^2 (.95;4)
Structural stability after OC2 :   29.95 < χ^2 (.95;22)

Manufacturing sector in the UK
1958-1986

Production Workers   Nonproduction Workers

δ_{10} : -0.150   (-1.94) δ_{20} : -0.259   (-1.33)
δ_{11} : -0.006   (-1.46) δ_{21} : -0.012   (-1.62)
δ_{12} : 0.002   (0.52) δ_{22} : -0.000   (0.05)
κ_1 : -0.302   (-0.81) κ_2 : 0.585   (0.64)
λ_{11} : 1.172   (2.00) λ_{21} : 2.647   (1.85)
λ_{12} : -0.653   (-1.88) λ_{22} : -1.224   (-1.44)
γ_{11} : 8.992   (2.38) γ_{21} : 0.209   (0.14)
γ_{12} : -0.521   (-1.93) γ_{22} : 11.449   (1.56)
β_1 : 2.929   (4.42) β_2 : -3.128   (-3.48)

TESTS
SB : 2.05   SB : 1.96

ARCH   ARCH
1   0.00   1   1.26
2   0.05   2   0.76
3   0.44   3   0.84
4   0.49   4   1.42

Overidentifying restrictions   :   11.47 < χ^2 (.95;8)
Symmetric linearity   :   9.63 > χ^2 (.95;4)
Structural stability after OC1 :   23.05 < χ^2 (.95;16)

[*] Asymptotic t-values are given within parentheses.
[**] Seasonal dummies have not been reported.

level for the Netherlands and for the UK.

The ARCH statistic has been suggested by Engle (1982) to test for autoregressive conditional heteroscedasticity in the residuals. ARCH has a chi-squared distribution with degrees of freedom equal to the number of autoregressive lags for which ARCH is being tested. According to this test there is no significant ARCH in the residuals for the two countries. This finding suggests that the firm's learning in the presence of a structural change in the forcing variables can indeed be modelled by adding dummy variables.

As we mentioned before, the symmetric linear model that has generally been applied in rational expectations factor demand analysis, is nested in our model. We compute Gallant's (1987) likelihood ratio (LR)-type statistic to test for symmetric linearity, while simultaneously imposing the following 4 restrictions : $\lambda_{12} = \lambda_{21}$; $\gamma_{12} = \gamma_{21}$; $\beta_1 = \beta_2 = 0$. For both the Netherlands and the UK, the test suggests that symmetric linearity must be rejected in favour of an asymmetric specification. Regime changes may have occurred after OC1 and OC2. Structural stability of the parameters has been tested using the Chow-type test suggested by Andrews and Fair (1987). Due to a lack of available data, we could not compute the impact of OC1 on parameter estimates for the Netherlands and the impact of OC2 on parameter estimates for the UK. The tests reject the hypothe-

sis that all the parameters for the UK (except OC1) and for the
Netherlands (except OC2) have undergone a structural change
after OC1 and OC2 respectively.

Least squares estimation applied to models with unobserved
expectational variables produces inconsistent estimates. But
there is, a trade off between efficiency and consistency. By
including more IVs in Ω_{t-1} GMM converges to nonlinear least
squares (NLS), which, apparently, leads to higher t-values. We
have chosen to restrict the number of IVs. Consequently, we
find relatively low t-values for the parameter estimates.

The (2x2)-matrix $\{\gamma_{ij}\}$ is found to be positive definite for both
countries. This is a sufficient (but not necessary) condition
for strictly convex adjustment costs. The estimated coefficients are plausible and in accordance with results of comparable research (e.g. Pindyck and Rotemberg (1983b), Shapiro
(1986)). Adjustment costs of nonproduction workers exceed
adjustment costs of production workers ($\gamma_{11} < \gamma_{22}$) whereas the
off-diagonal interrelated costs (γ_{12}, γ_{21}) do not play an important role (and therefore are usually restricted to zero prior to
estimation).

The parameter estimates measuring the asymmetry of the adjustment cost funtion (β_1, β_2) are significantly different from zero,
for the Netherlands and the UK. The results are intuitively
plausible and add an extra empirical element to the discussion

of unbalanced cyclical changes in (un)employment between the two types of labour. The costs of firing production workers are low compared to the costs of hiring ($\beta_1 > 0$). Asymmetric adjustment costs yield different speeds of adjustment during economic upswings (hirings exceeding firings) and recessions (firings exceeding hirings). Production workers are more easily fired during recessions than hired during upswings.

Firing costs exceed hiring costs for nonproduction workers ($\beta_2 < 0$). Costs that a firm faces for having a personnel management and training department that may be considered as on the job investment explain why firing costs exceed hiring costs for nonproduction workers. The empirical finding that firms often hoard nonproduction workers should be considered to arise from lower overall adjustment costs of production workers, not with standing the "anticyclical" differences between hiring and firing costs of the two types of labour.

6.4 Factor Demand with Asymmetric Adjustment Costs

In the previous section we assumed that firms maximize their expected real present value of profits by optimally choosing the input level of employment conditional on current information available and the capital stock being predetermined. However, in the literature on the demand for production factors under uncertainty it has often been argued that the current level of employment and the current capital stock are determined simultaneously (e.g. Meese (1980), Epstein and Denny (1983), Pindyck and Rotemberg (1983 a,b), Kokkelenberg (1984), Epstein and Yatchew (1985)).

In this section capital is assumed to be a decision variable too. We also assume capital to be quasi-fixed, that is, when the firm alters the capital stock it faces adjustment costs. Kydland and Prescott (1982) noted that the failure of overidentifying restriction tests in linear rational expectations adjustment costs models arises from dynamic misspecification. They argued that such models cannot possibly explain complicated gestation lags of the firm's capital, which arise from time to build considerations. Rossi (1987) compared the two models and presented empirical evidence in favour of the time to build model using two different US data sets. We investigate whether the adjustment costs model is also found to be inadequate when the adjustment cost function is asymmetric.

In analogy with the previous section we assume that the costs of scrapping capital can differ from investment costs, i.e. adjustment costs of capital may be asymmetric.

Marginal productivity of factor input, X_{it}, at period t, where $X_{1t} = N_{1t}$, $X_{2t} = N_{2t}$ and $X_{3t} = K_t$, is now modelled as follows

$$MP(X_{it}) = \alpha_i - \sum_{j=1}^{3} \lambda_{ij} X_{it} + \xi_{it}, \quad i=1,2,3. \qquad (VI.1)'$$

Marginal asymmetric adjustment costs of factor i become

$$MAC(\Delta X_{it}) = \beta_i(\exp(\beta_i \Delta X_{it})-1) + \sum_{j=1}^{3} \gamma_{ij} \Delta X_{jt}, \quad i=1,2,3, \quad (VI.2)'$$

where α_i, β_i, γ_{ij} and λ_{ij} are constant parameters, and ξ_{it} represent the unforeseen stochastic productivity shocks.

We assume that the firm faces linear variable costs that are proportional to factor input at each time t. In order to maximise the real present value of its expected profit stream the firm will make contingency plans for labour and capital satisfying the Euler conditions

$$MP(X_{it}) - MAC(\Delta X_{it}) - P_{it} + \tau \, E[MAC(\Delta X_{it+1}) + dP_{t+1} | \Omega_t] = 0,$$

$$(IV.3)'$$

where $P_t = (W_{1t}, W_{2t}, Q_t)$, Q_t is the real price of capital, d is a diagonal (3×3)-matrix $(0;0;(1-\delta))'$, and δ denotes the depreciation rate of capital which we assume to be constant. We used a value of 5% per year in the empirical analysis. After substitution of the realized values for the unobserved expectations in (VI.3)', the Euler equations lead to the following model

$$\begin{bmatrix} \delta_{01} \\ \delta_{02} \\ \delta_{03} \end{bmatrix} CONST + \begin{bmatrix} \delta_{11} \\ \delta_{12} \\ \delta_{13} \end{bmatrix} OC1 + \begin{bmatrix} \delta_{21} \\ \delta_{22} \\ \delta_{23} \end{bmatrix} OC2 - \begin{bmatrix} 1 & 0 & 0 \\ 0 & 1 & 0 \\ 0 & 0 & 1 \end{bmatrix} \begin{bmatrix} W_{1t} \\ W_{2t} \\ Q_t \end{bmatrix} + \begin{bmatrix} 0 \\ 0 \\ \tau(1-\delta) \end{bmatrix} Q_{t+1}$$

$$- \begin{bmatrix} \lambda_{11} & \lambda_{12} & \lambda_{13} \\ \lambda_{21} & \lambda_{22} & \lambda_{23} \\ \lambda_{31} & \lambda_{32} & \lambda_{33} \end{bmatrix} \begin{bmatrix} N_{1t} \\ N_{2t} \\ K_t \end{bmatrix} + \begin{bmatrix} \gamma_{11} & 0 & 0 \\ 0 & \gamma_{22} & 0 \\ 0 & 0 & \gamma_{33} \end{bmatrix} \begin{bmatrix} \Delta N_{1t}-\tau\Delta N_{1t+1} \\ \Delta N_{2t}-\tau\Delta N_{2t+1} \\ \Delta K_t-\tau\Delta K_{t+1} \end{bmatrix}$$

$$- \begin{bmatrix} \beta_1(\exp(\beta_1\Delta N_{1t})-\tau \, \exp(\beta_1\Delta N_{1t+1})) \\ \beta_2(\exp(\beta_2\Delta N_{2t})-\tau \, \exp(\beta_2\Delta N_{2t+1})) \\ \beta_3(\exp(\beta_3\Delta K_t)-\tau \, \exp(\beta_3\Delta K_{t+1})) \end{bmatrix} = \begin{bmatrix} u_{1t+1} - \xi_{1t} \\ u_{2t+1} - \xi_{2t} \\ u_{3t+1} - \xi_{3t} \end{bmatrix}. \quad (IV.4)'$$

Table VI.4 : COINTEGRATION TESTS : THE FORCING VARIABLES ARE $\{W_{1t}, W_{2t}, Q_t\}$.

Cointegrating regressions for the manufacturing sector in the Netherlands[*]
1971.I - 1984.IV

	CONST	OC1	OC2	TREND	W_{1t}	W_{2t}	Q_t	$\overline{R}^2$	CRDW	ADF
N_{1t}	0.67 (3.68)	0.00 (0.00)	0.04 (2.16)		-0.51 (-2.62)	-0.70 (-3.91)	1.51 (7.37)	0.97	0.41	-2.12
	1.64 (11.72)	-0.07 (-5.65)	0.03 (2.80)	-0.01 (-10.16)	0.73 (4.46)	-0.52 (-5.17)	-0.49 (-2.15)	0.99	0.95	-3.36
N_{2t}	0.56 (2.92)	0.14 (7.52)	0.03 (1.77)		-1.59 (-7.84)	0.44 (2.33)	1.46 (6.77)	0.94	1.06	-3.20
	1.56 (10.39)	0.07 (5.40)	0.02 (2.08)	-0.01 (-9.79)	-0.31 (-1.78)	0.62 (5.63)	-0.62 (-2.53)	0.98	0.70	-3.78
K_t	1.70 (13.24)	-0.04 (-3.43)	-0.02 (-1.77)		0.51 (3.74)	0.42 (3.31)	-1.58 (-10.89)	0.97	0.77	-2.49
	0.94 (13.52)	0.01 (1.66)	-0.02 (-2.85)	0.01 (15.92)	-0.45 (-5.57)	0.28 (5.58)	-0.01 (-0.11)	1.00	0.92	-3.77

Cointegrating regressions for the manufacturing sector in the UK
1955 - 1986

	CONST	OC1	OC2	TREND	W_{1t}	W_{2t}	Q_t	$\overline{R}^2$	CRDW	ADF
N_{1t}	1.47 (4.09)	-0.10 (-4.58)	-0.06 (-2.10)		0.74 (2.87)	-0.97 (-4.81)	-0.18 (-0.41)	0.96	0.85	-3.80
	1.88 (4.66)	-0.15 (-4.69)	-0.04 (-1.61)	0.02 (1.92)	0.65 (2.60)	-1.30 (-5.06)	-0.42 (-0.96)	0.97	1.15	-5.01
N_{2t}	0.54 (0.78)	-0.16 (-3.53)	-0.06 (-1.13)		2.39 (4.73)	-1.89 (-4.78)	0.03 (0.04)	0.73	1.03	-3.27
	1.67 (2.28)	-0.28 (-4.81)	-0.02 (-0.45)	0.04 (2.86)	2.15 (4.72)	-2.78 (-5.94)	0.04 (2.86)	0.79	1.28	-4.66
K_t	-0.35 (-1.47)	0.05 (3.47)	-0.02 (-1.35)		0.78 (4.51)	0.02 (0.16)	0.54 (1.83)	0.99	1.66	-3.38
	0.33 (-2.40)	-0.02 (-1.88)	-0.00 (-0.18)	0.03 (9.27)	0.63 (7.43)	-0.51 (-5.90)	0.14 (1.00)	1.00	1.62	-4.03

[*]   Asymptotic t-values are given within parentheses. OC1 = 1 for the period 1973.IV - 1984.IV
      and 1974-1986, OC2 = 1 for the period 1979.II - 1984.IV and 1979-1986 in the regressions
      for the Netherlands and the UK respectively.
[**]   Seasonal dummies are not reported.

Production and nonproduction real wage costs and the real price of capital are now the forcing variables in the system. Therefore, we alternatively test for cointegration between decision variables N_{1t}, N_{2t} and K_t on the one hand, and W_{1t}, W_{2t} and Q_t on the other hand. From the results, presented in table VI.4, we may draw the following conclusions. Some doubt is cast upon the existence of a long run equilibrium relationship between real factor prices and production employment and capital in the Netherlands, whereas the test of cointegration on nonproduction employment in the Netherlands and the UK manufacturing factor inputs seems to be only marginally significant. A possible explantion for this finding may be the coexistence of stochastic trends (real factor prices) and deterministic trends (e.g. technological innovations). Hence, we also test for cointegration when a linear deterministic trend is included in the regression equation. The inclusion of a trend removes the random walk behaviour from the long run equilibria. Consequently, a linear time trend was added to the first order conditions (VI.4)'.

Note that in equation (VI.4)' we have restricted the matrix $\{\gamma_{ij}\}$ to be diagonal prior to estimation. The reason is threefold. First, it is consistent with the literature on dynamic factor demand. Second, the findings of the previous section partly suggest it. Third, due to the computational complexity and limited number of observations, only a small number of structural parameters can be estimated. Also the sets of IVs have been chosen in accordance with the information set Ω_t of the extended model.

The information set for the Netherlands has been extended by including a linear time trend, whereas the lagged levels of production and nonproduction employment and capital have been replaced by one period lagged first differences of these variables. The number of IVs in the information set for the Netherlands then equals 17. In the information set for the UK a linear trend has been included as well. The one and two periods lagged decision variables (L_1, L_2, K) have been replaced by one period lagged first differences, and the one period lagged first differenced real price of capital has also been added. Then the number of IVs for the UK is 12. GMM parameter estimates of the asymmetric adjustment cost function and model specification tests are given in table VI.5. The estimates of other structural parameters have not been presented, but can be obtained from the author upon request.

There is significant evidence for the presence of first order ARCH in the residuals of nonproduction workers in the Netherlands. The SB statistic does not point at any significant nonstationarity in the residuals for the Netherlands. In the model for the Netherlands the overidentifying restrictions are not rejected. Linearity (H_0 : $\beta_i = 0$, i=1,2,3) is rejected.

Table VI.5 : GMM estimates of adjustment costs parameters and tests*

Manufacturing sector in the Netherlands
1971.IV - 1984.IV

Production Workers	Nonproduction Workers	Capital
γ_{11} : 50.76 (3.07)	γ_{22} : 75.66 (1.85)	γ_{33} : 83.05 (2.73)
β_1 : 7.48 (5.85)	β_2 : -9.08 (-3.74)	β_3 : -9.48 (-5.22)

TESTS

SB : 1.82	SB : 2.32	SB : 2.26

ARCH		ARCH		ARCH	
1	0.31	1	8.53	1	1.45
2	0.84	2	7.27	2	2.68
3	0.96	3	7.98	3	5.32
4	1.37	4	8.45	4	5.89

Overidentifying restrictions	:	$15.64 < \chi^2$ (.95;15)
Linearity	:	$15.35 > \chi^2$ (.95;3)
Structural stability after OC2	:	$40.92 < \chi^2$ (.95;33)

Manufacturing sector in the UK
1958 - 1986

Production Workers	Nonproduction Workers	Capital
γ_{11} : 9.61 (1.95)	γ_{22} : 7.14 (1.22)	γ_{33} : 97.16 (1.47)
β_1 : 3.18 (3.85)	β_2 : -2.47 (-2.71)	β_3 : -11.06 (-2.63)

TESTS

SB : 1.95	SB : 1.81	SB : 1.59

ARCH		ARCH		ARCH	
1	1.77	1	0.69	1	0.58
2	1.57	2	0.94	2	2.47
3	2.77	3	1.48	3	3.31
4	4.91	4	1.49	4	3.22

Overidentifying restrictions	:	$17.48 > \chi^2$ (.95;9)
Linearity	:	$15.64 > \chi^2$ (.95;3)
Structural stability after OC1	:	$38.41 > \chi^2$ (.95;24)

* Asymptotic t-values are given within parentheses.

There is no evidence in the data for the Netherlands that the parameters have undergone a structural change after OC2.

The SB statistic points at the presence of nonstationarity in the residuals for capital in the UK (although the power of this test is low). The over-identifying restrictions and the structural stability are rejected at a 5 percent level, but not at a 1 percent level. Linearity is rejected for the UK data as well.

The estimated value of UK's γ_{22} is unexpectedly low compared with γ_{11}. Although this result is not significant, it is inconsistent with the results presented in the previous section. The estimate of asymmetry adjustment costs parameter of capital, β_3, is negative for the Netherlands and for the UK. Therefore, scrapping of capital will take more time than building up new capital. The firm retains from scrapping capital during recessions, whereas the firm more quickly takes investment decisions during periods of an economic upswing.

6.5 Conclusions

In this chapter we developed and analysed dynamic demand models for the profit maximising firm with asymmetric adjustment costs under uncertainty. Sections 2 and 3 have been concerned with decisions to employ production and nonproduction workers when the capital stock is predetermined. In section 4, the firm has been assumed to jointly determine the optimal level of labour and capital. The models have been applied and tested, using quarterly time series data of the manufacturing sector in the Netherlands for the period 1971.I - 1984.IV, and annual data for the manufacturing sector in the UK for the period 1955-1986.

To summarize, the following conclusions were reached.

1. Unexpected shocks in the (exogenous) environment of the firm give rise to step changes in the decision rules of the firm, and may well induce ARCH in the residuals due to increased uncertainty which can result from a structural change in the process of the forcing variables.

2. When employment decisions are assumed to be taken conditionally on the available capital stock, the employment of production and nonproduction workers respectively is cointegrated with capital and production and nonproduction real wage costs. However, if decisions on production factor inputs are simultaneously taken, there is no significant evidence for the existence of a long run relationship between factor inputs on the one hand and real factor prices on the other hand. There is however evidence for the coexistence of stochastic trends (real input prices) and deterministic trends (e.g. technological innovations).

3. Hiring costs exceed firing costs of production workers.

4. Firing costs exceed hiring costs of nonproduction workers.

5. Scrapping costs exceed investment costs of capital.

By and large, we may conclude that the asymmetric adjustment costs model is more appropriate for the data we analysed than the linear quadratic model. Moreover, we feel that the asymmetric model performs better than the symmetric one when the capital stock is assumed to be predetermined. A more extended comparison of time-to-build models of capital with asymmetric adjustment costs models will be the subject of future research.

CHAPTER 7 : CONCLUSIONS AND SUMMARY

7.1 Conclusions and Summary

In this dissertation we examine labour demand from an employer's point of view. Manufacturing firms are assumed to be represented through an enterprising agent called "the representative firm", who maximizes the expected real present value of future profits. The firm is assumed to form future expectations about the economic environment as accurately as possible, using all relevant information currently available, in order to develop an optimal intertemporal employment policy. Realizations of labour input plans are nevertheless stochastic because of unanticipated shocks in the economic environment of the firm.

The firm's optimal level of employment may change because market conditions change, for example through shifts in product demand, input price ratios, or due to technological innovation. However, rapid adjustment of the work force to a new target level can be very expensive if not impossible. Adjustment will be carried out gradually. As a consequence, labour demand is dynamic. Both factor and output markets are assumed to be perfectly competitive.

Initially, we impose a rather stringent mathematical structure on the relevant economic theory. This enables us to derive labour demand equations that are susceptible to empirical analysis, to estimate behavioural parameters and to assess their intuitive plausibility, and to test overidentifying parameter restrictions implied by economic theory. We gradually relax some of the theoretical restrictions in order to overcome some of the shortcomings of the linear symmetric labour demand model.

Chapter 2 presents a prototype labour demand model describing the stationary serial correlation structure of quarterly data on blue and white collar employment and real wage costs in the Dutch manufacturing sector for the period 1971.I to 1984.IV. This chapter draws heavily upon Sargent (1978). The theoretical contribution of chapter 2 consists of insights into the identification of the structural parameters of the underlying economic theory obtained from a closed form solution of a linear rational expectations demand model for blue and white collar labour in which adjustment costs play a dominant role.

In chapter 3 some refinements are proposed with respect to the functional forms of production and adjustment costs specifications. The mathematical expressions of both specifications are extended so as to allow for interrelatedness between the input decisions of blue and white collar labour. Nonstationarity of economic time series are considered to be essential part of the theoretical model. In chapter 3 capital is assumed to be predetermined. Capital is modelled as a forcing variable with respect to employment decisions, and nonstationarity in the capital stock is used to explain nonstationarity in labour demand. The resulting dynamic labout demand model is used to describe the nonstationary correlation structure of quarterly data of the total number of weekly hours worked by blue and white collar labour in the Dutch manufacturing sector for the same period as the previous chapter.

Chapter 4 discusses the multivariate stochastic control problem of the firm, where capital and labour are assumed to be determined simultaneously. In particular, we examine the impact of structural changes in the process of exogenous variables on factor demand both theoretically and empirically. Chapter 4 also focusses on cointegrating properties of production factors and real input prices.

Ever since the first dynamic analysis of planning production and work force (Holt et.al. 1960) the costs of hiring and firing labour have been modelled jointly through a quadratic function of changes in employment. This symmetry hypothesis implies that the costs of hiring a number of workers are equal to the costs of firing the same number of workers. Chapter 5 examines the appropriateness of quadratic adjustment costs of labout in dynamic labour demand models. We interviewed personnel managers of DSM Chemicals, FOKKER Aircrafts, HOOGOVENS Steel, VENDEX International and VOLVO Cars. The interviews concentrate mainly on these firms' decisions to change their productive work force and the costs that arise from these changes.

Also in chapter 5, we introduce, estimate and test a generalized function which allows for asymmetric adjustment costs and measures the difference between hiring costs and firing costs. In chapter 6 the asymmetric function has been implemented into two dynamic labour demand models. In one model, capital is assumed to be predetermined when employment decisions are taken. The other model assumes that investment and employment decisions are taken simultaneously. Econometric analysis is also presented using time series data of Dutch and U.K. blue and white collar manufacturing employment.

Summarizing, the most important conclusions that may be drawn from this dissertation are the following.

1: The empirical results confirm the well known fact that blue collar labour is easier to adjust to a new target level than white collar labour, due to lower hiring and firing costs.

2: It is shown that interrelation of demand equations for various production factors, equations that are derived from a quadratic objective function, does not emerge from trade-off in costs or substitution between production factors. In such models the interrelation can only result from the way in which firms react to random shocks by adjusting the input mix.

3: The (dynamic) relation between blue and white collar labour is as follows. As a result of higher adjustment costs during an economic depression a firm will hoard white collar labour, blue collar workers substituting for white collar workers, thus upgrading the firm's work force. On the other hand, when more blue collar workers are hired, more supervising white collar workers are needed. Consequently, we may state that white collar labour is complementary to blue collar labour, whereas blue collar labour can be replaced by white collar labour.

4: The gradual learning about the nature of structural changes may cause systematic patterns in the disturbances of the demand equations. Such misspecification can be detected by testing for autocorrelation and ARCH.

5: When manufacturing employment decisions are assumed to be conditional on the available capital stock, blue and white collar employment are found to be cointegrated with capital and the real wage costs of the two types of labour. If decisions on inputs of blue collar labour, white collar labour and capital are assumed to be taken simultaneously, there is significant evidence for the existence of a long run relationship between factor inputs on the one hand and stochastic trends (real input prices) and deterministic trends (technological innovations) on the other hand.

6: Adjustment costs of labour cannot be represented appropriately by a quadratic function. The asymmetric adjustment costs model fits our data better than the traditional linear-quadratic labour demand model. Moreover, hiring costs exceed firing costs of blue collar workers, whereas firing costs exceed hiring costs for white collar workers, both in the Dutch and U.K. manufacturing sectors.

These are important findings, which should be taken into account when examining labour demand from an employer's point of view. But these results are also meaningful for macroeconomic modelling of labour demand. Broer (1985) presents a theoretical and empirical macroeconomic analysis of aggregate firm behaviour, based on putty-putty and putty-clay models of capital and labour inputs, using annual Dutch business and manufacturing data. The results of our study might be used to supplement Broer's study in the sense that we provide deeper insight into parameter identification of quadratic models with and without assuming capital being predetermined, and that asymmetric specifications of adjustment costs structures are appropriate for modelling dynamic labour demand.

In this book effects of possible substitution between hours worked and persons employed have not been considered. De Regt (1988) examines the hypothesis that the number of hours worked varies proportionally with standard working time, and that substitution takes place between the number of workers and average working time. For empirical analysis annual data are used for Dutch manufacturing aggregate employment from 1954 to 1982. De Regt argues that the relation between the number of workers and the average working time crucially depends upon the elasticity of capital substitution with respect to labour services, and finds that a 10 percent reduction of standard working time will increase employment by 4 percent. However, elasticities of substitution will differ between blue and white collar labour. Moreover, if firms do not plan their workforce and the optimal working hours simultaneously, the dynamic structure of employment does not depend upon the number of hours worked.

Analysis of dynamic labour demand should be extended in these directions if well-considered answers are to be given to questions concerning the effects of introducing shorter working hours.

Further research is also needed to investigate which dynamic relations exist between production technologies, technological innovation and factor inputs, since neither the growth of capital stock as a proxy, nor deterministic trends model technical progress adequately (see Nickell and Symons (1987)). Finally, extending the dynamic labour demand model may prove fruitful in modelling the agent's learning process after unforeseen shocks with time varying parameters, as suggested by Bray and Savin (1986).

APPENDICES

In (II.15) the vector of parameters

$$\beta = (\mu_{11}, \mu_{12}, \mu_{21}, \mu_{22}, \rho_1, \rho_2, \alpha_{12}, \alpha_{22}, \beta_1, \beta_2)$$

is an estimable function of

$$\theta = (\mu_{11}, \mu_{12}, \mu_{21}, \mu_{22}, \rho_1, \rho_2, \delta_1, \delta_2, \lambda_1, \lambda_2)$$

say

$$g(\theta) = \beta.$$

If we have a consistent estimator of θ, $\hat{\theta}$, with large sample distribution $\sqrt{T} (\hat{\theta} - \theta_0) \underset{a}{\sim} N (0, \Omega(\theta_0))$

where Ω is the covariance matrix of $\hat{\theta}$ evaluated at the original true parameters θ_0 (Gouriéroux et.al. 1985), then β can be estimated by

$$\hat{\beta} = g(\hat{\theta}).$$

Furthermore,

$$\sqrt{T} (\hat{\beta} - \beta_0) \underset{a}{\sim} N (0, Q \Omega Q')$$

where $Q = \dfrac{\partial g(\theta)}{\partial \theta'}$.

143

APPENDIX A.2 : PROOFS OF PROPOSITIONS OF CHAPTER THREE

Proof of Proposition 1 :

Let $\mathbf{S} = \begin{bmatrix} S & 0 \\ 0 & S \end{bmatrix}$, where S is a regular (2x2)-matrix S such that

$S^{-1}\tilde{A}S$ is uppertriangular with eigenvalues μ_1 and μ_2 of $\tilde{A}$ on the

diagonal.

Then $\mathbf{S}^{-1} \mathbf{A} \mathbf{S} = \begin{bmatrix} S^{-1} & 0 \\ 0 & S^{-1} \end{bmatrix} \begin{bmatrix} 0 & S \\ -\tau^{-1}S & \tilde{A}S \end{bmatrix} = \begin{bmatrix} 0 & I_2 \\ -\tau^{-1}I_2 & S^{-1}\tilde{A}S \end{bmatrix}.$

Now, the characteristic polynomial of $\mathbf{S}^{-1} \mathbf{A} \mathbf{S}$ and con-

sequently of A equals $(-\lambda^2 + \mu_1\lambda - \tau^{-1})(-\lambda^2 + \mu_2\lambda - \tau^{-1})$.

If $\mu_1 \neq \mu_2$ S can be chosen such that $S^{-1}\tilde{A}S$ is diagonal. Then

the columns of S are the eigenvectors of $\tilde{A}$.

Proof of Proposition 3 :

Redefine $H^{-1} = (SC_{22})^{-1} \Lambda_2^{-1} SC_{22}$, $\Gamma_1 = (\tau B)^{-1}$,

and $Q_S = \sum_{i=0}^{\infty} H^{-i-1} \Gamma_1 \tilde{R}^i$.

Then $H = (SC_{22})^{-1} \Lambda_2 SC_{22}$ and $HQ_S - Q_S\tilde{R} = \Gamma_1$ ◆

$\text{vec}(HQ_S) - \text{vec}(Q_S\tilde{R}) = \text{vec}(\Gamma_1)$ ◆

$(I_2 \otimes H)\text{vec}(Q_S) - (\tilde{R}^T \otimes I_2)\text{vec}(Q_S) = \text{vec}(\Gamma_1)$ ◆

$\text{vec}(Q_S) = [I_2 \otimes H - \tilde{R}^T \otimes I_2]^{-1} \text{vec}(\Gamma_1).$

144

APPENDIX A.3 : PARTIAL ADJUSTMENT, ERROR CORRECTION AND COINTEGRATION

Let $x_t = (\ell_t, k_t)'$ being a 2-vector of instruments available to the firm to maximize its real present value of profits (2.4) and $x_t \sim I(1)$. We can write x_t as a partial adjustment mechanism, say

$$\Delta x_t = M (x_{t-1} - x^*) \tag{II.1}$$

with $M = \Lambda_1 - I$ and $x^* = (\Lambda_1 - I) \sum_{i=0}^{\infty} (\Lambda_1)^{i+1} B^{-1} p_{t+i}^*$, where (for the case of simplicity) the matrices A and B in (2.1) and (2.2) respectively are assumed to be diagonal and the real discount factor, τ, is assumed to be one (quarterly data), and $p_{t+i}^* = E(p_{t+i} \mid \Omega_t)$ is a 2-vector of expectations at time t of future values of exogenous variables.

We assume that p_t follows an AR(2) process with a unit root and drift, say,

$$\Delta p_{t+i} = p_0 + Q \Delta p_{t+i-1} + \xi_{t+i} . \tag{II.2}$$

Then the expectation p_{t+i}^* is as follows (cf. Nickell 1985) :

$$p_{t+i}^* = p_{t-1} + \tilde{p}_0 + (I + Q^{i+1})(I - Q)^{-1} \Delta p_t \tag{II.3}$$

where $\tilde{p}_0 = \sum_{j=0}^{i-1} (i-j) Q^j p_0$,

Substituting (II.2) and (II.3) into (II.1) we get

$$\Delta x_t = x_0 + M x_{t-1} + B^{-1} \Lambda_1 M^{-1} p_{t-1} + \tilde{Q} \Delta p_t + \xi_t^x$$

where $\tilde{Q} = B^{-1} \left[((\Lambda_1 Q)^{-1} - I)^{-1} - (\Lambda_1^{-1} - I)^{-1} \right]^{-1}$, and x_0 is a scalar.

Consequently, we have

$$\left[I : B^{-1} \Lambda_1 M^{-2} \right] (x_{t-1}, \ p_{t-1})' \sim I(0) .$$

According to Granger's Representation Theorem (Engle and Granger (1987)) this implies that x_t and p_t cointegrate.

APPENDIX A.4 : FORECAST ERRORS, EXPECTATIONAL ERRORS AND RANDOM

SHOCKS

The model with a quadratic production function and an adjustment
cost function of the general quadratic exponential form given in
equation (VI.2) yields the following expectational errors :

(1) $u_{t+1} = -\tau\gamma(\Delta x_{t+1} - E_t[\Delta x_{t+1}]) - \tau\beta(\exp(\beta\Delta x_{t+1})$

$\qquad - E_t[\exp(\beta\Delta x_{t+1})])$,

where x_t is a decision variable of the firm, γ is the adjustment
parameter of the quadratic term, and β is the adjustment parameter, which expresses the asymmetry of the adjustment cost
function, τ is the constant real discount rate, and $E_t =$
$E[\cdot|\Omega_t]$, with Ω_t being the information set at time t.

In order to trace the effects of a structural break, we make an
additional distributional assumption. Let

(2) $x_{t+1} = E_t[x_{t+1}] + \epsilon_{t+1}$, or $\Delta x_{t+1} = E_t[\Delta x_{t+1}] + \epsilon_{t+1}$,

since $E_t[x_t] = x_t$, and where ϵ_{t+1} is the forecast error at t+1.

(3) We assume that $\epsilon_{t+1} \sim N(0, \sigma_{t+1}^2)$.

If during a time interval (e.g. the sample period) no structural
change occurs in the slope or in the variance of the decision
variable x, the expectational error, u_{t+1}, is a white noise process. This can be shown as follows.

From equations (1) and (2) we can derive

(4) $u_{t+1} = -\tau\gamma\epsilon_{t+1} - \tau\beta(\exp(\beta E_t[\Delta x_{t+1}]+\beta\epsilon_{t+1})$

$\qquad\qquad E_t[\exp(\beta E_t[\Delta x_{t+1}]+\beta\epsilon_{t+1})]).$

From (3) it follows that $\exp(\epsilon_{t+1})$ is lognormally distributed with zero mean and variance σ^2_{t+1}. Then (4) becomes

(5) $u_{t+1} = -\tau\gamma\epsilon_{t+1} - \tau\beta(\exp(\beta E_t[\Delta x_{t+1}])\exp(\beta\epsilon_{t+1}))$

$\qquad\qquad -\tau\beta(\exp(\beta E_t[\Delta x_{t+1}]\exp(\tfrac{1}{2}\beta^2_t \sigma^2_{t+1})),$

where $_t\sigma^2_{t+1} = E_t[\sigma^2_{t+1}]$.

Since $_t\sigma^2_{t+1} = \sigma^2$, say, the unconditional expectation of u_{t+1} equals zero, that is

(6) $E[u_{t+1}] = 0,$

since $E[\epsilon_{t+1}] = 0$ and $E[\exp(\beta\epsilon_{t+1})] = E_t[\exp(\beta\epsilon_{t+1})] = \tfrac{1}{2}\beta^2\sigma^2,$

and

(7) $E[u^2_{t+1}] = \tau^2(\gamma^2\sigma^2 + \beta^2\exp(2\beta^2\sigma^2) - \beta^2\exp(\beta^2\sigma^2) + 2\gamma\beta v^2_{t+1})$

where $v^2_{t+1} = E[\epsilon_{t+1}(\exp(\beta\Delta x_{t+1}) - E_t[\exp(\beta\Delta x_{t+1})])],$

so that u_{t+1} is white noise.

Now consider an unanticipated step change in the slope of x

occurring between t and t+1, whereas the forecast error variance remains unaffected, that is

$$\Delta x_{t+1} = c + E_t[\Delta x_{t+1}] + \epsilon_{t+1} \; ; \; E[\epsilon_{t+1}^2] = E_t[\epsilon_{t+1}^2] = \sigma^2.$$

Then

$$(6') \quad E[u_{t+1}] = -\tau\gamma c - \tau\beta \; \exp(\beta E_t[\Delta x_{t+1}])\cdot \exp(\tfrac{1}{2}\beta\sigma^2)\cdot(\exp(\beta c)-1).$$

and

$$(7') \quad E[u_{t+1}^2] = \tau^2(\gamma^2\sigma^2 + \beta^2 \; \exp(2c)(\exp(2\beta^2\sigma^2) - \exp(\beta^2\sigma^2) +$$
$$+ \; 2\gamma\beta v_{t+1}^2)$$

Consequently, when the forecast error is normally distributed an unexpected shock which changes the slope of the decision variable x_t but not its variance, leads to a step change in both the unconditional mean and the variance of the expectational error u_{t+1}.

Analogously, an unexpected exogenous shock (e.g. increased uncertainty) which does not change the slope of x_t but persistently changes the forecast error variance, also leads to a step change in the unconditional mean of the expectational error u and its variance.

APPENDIX A.5 : Data Sources and Definitions.

SOURCES OF THE QUARTERLY DUTCH MANUFACTURING (SBI 2/3) DATA

The base year of all prices and indices is 1980.

L^*, L_1, L_2 : The total numbers (in thousands) of blue collar workers (L_1) and white collar workers (L_2) have been computed from quarterly indices of total manufacturing employment (L^*), obtained from the Centraal Bureau voor de Statistiek (CBS), Algemene Industrie Statistiek, and manufacturing total aggregate numbers and the ratio of blue and white collar workers which have been interpolated from the CBS Loonstruktuur Onderzoek 1972 and the Arbeidskrachtentelling 1975, 1977, 1979, 1981, and 1983.

H_1, H_2 : Average weekly working hours including overtime hours for blue collar workers (H_1) and white collar workers (H_2) have been obtained from the CBS Halfjaarlijks Loononderzoek. These series are six-monthly data which have been interpolated.

N_1, N_2 : Total number of weekly hours worked by blue collar workers (N_1) and white collar workers (N_2) : $N_i = L_i * H_i$, i = 1,2.

Py : Producers price index of domestic sales; Producenten Prijsindexcijfers van de Binnenlandse Afzet van de Nederlandse Industrie (SBI 2/3) are unpublished data which have been kindly provided by CBS.

W^*, W_1, W_2 : Gross hourly wage costs for blue collar workers (Pl_1) and white collar workers (Pl_2) have been computed from the CBS Halfjaarlijks Loononderzoek, the CBS Driejaarlijks Loonkosten Onderzoek, started in 1972, and the quarterly index of wage costs in current prices (W^*) obtained from the CBS Kwartaalonderzoek Verdiende Lonen. Real hourly wage costs (W_1, W_2) have been obtained by deflating Pl_1 and Pl_2 respectively by Py.

Y : Index manufacturing output in constant prices, obtained from CBS Nationale Rekeningen.

K, Q   : Net capital stock (K) has been computed from annual
                manufacturing capital stock data which are used in
                the VINSEC model of the Centraal Plan Bureau (CPB),
                and from quarterly aggregate data of capital stocks
                used in the CPB model KOMPAS. The real price of
                capital has been obtained by deflating the price
                index of manufacturing investment goods in current
                prices (Pk) by Py.

R3L, YGB   : Rate on three months loans to local authorities
                (R3L) and the yield of long term government bonds
                (YGB) for the Netherlands have been obtained from
                OECD Main Economic Indicators.

NUR   : Rate of registered unemployment in the Netherlands
                (NUR) obtained from the Ministerie van Sociale
                Zaken en Werkgelegenheid.

SOURCES OF THE ANNUAL U.K. MANUFACTURING DATA

The base year of all prices and indices is 1980.
The following main data sources were used :

BB	:	Blue Book
DEG	:	Department of Employment Gazette
ETAS	:	Economic Trend Annual Supplement
HABLS	:	Historical Abstract of British Labour Statistic
MM	:	Mendis L. and J. Muellbauer (1984), British Manufacturing Productivity 19855-1983 : Measurement Problems, Oil Shocks, and Thatcher Effects, CEPR Discussion Paper No. 34.

N_1, N_2 : Total (full time and part time) number of production workers (N_1) and nonproduction workers (N_2) have been computed from the ETAS total number of employees in U.K. manufacturing, and DEG employment shares.

Y, Py : Index of total manufacturing output (Y), and producers price index of home sales of all manufactured products (Py) have been obtained from ETAS.

W_1, W_2 : Index of real weekly earnings of full time production workers (W_1) and nonproduction workers (W_2) have been obtained by deflating gross weekly earnings of manual and nonmanual workers respectively (pre-1970 data : HABLS; from 1970 on data : New Earnings Survey in DEG) by Py.

K, Q : The gross capital stock at constant prices (K) have been obtained from BB for data from 1963 and from MM for pre-1963 data. The real price of capital (Q) has been obtained by dividing the series for manufacturing investment in current and constant prices obtained from ETAS and deflating this series by Py.

Pm : Producer price index of materials and fuel purchased by manufacturing industry (ETAS).

REFERENCES

Andrews, D.W.K. and R.C. Fair (1988), "Inference in Nonlinear Econometric Models with Structural Change", Review of Economic Studies 55, 615-639.

Blanchard, O.J. and C.M. Kahn (1980), "The Solution of Linear Difference Models under Rational Expectations", Econometrica 48, 1305-1311.

Bray, M.M. and N.E. Savin (1986), "Rational Expectations Equilibria, Learning and Model Specification", Econometrica 54, 1129-1160.

Berndt, E.R., M.A. Fuss, and L. Waverman (1979), "A Dynamic Model of Costs of Adjustment and Interrelated Factor Demands with an Empirical Application to Energy Demand in U.S. Manufacturing", Institute for Policy Analysis, University of Toronto, Working Paper 7925.

Broer, D.P. (1985), "Neoclassical Theory and Empirical Models of Aggregate Firm Behaviour", Ph.D. Thesis, Erasmus University, Rotterdam.

Burgess, S. (1988), "Employment Adjustment in U.K. Manufacturing", Economic Journal 98, 81-103.

Burgess, S. and J.J. Dolado (1988), "Intertemporal Rules with Variable Speed of Adjustment : An Application to U.K. Manufacturing Employment", Economic Journal, forthcoming.

Chamberlain, G. (1982) : "Multivariate Regression Models for Panel Data", Journal of Econometrics, 18, 5-46.

Chow, C.C. and Ph.J. Reny (1985), "On Two Methods for Solving and Estimating Linear Simultaneous Equations under Rational Expectations", Journal of Economic Dynamics and Control 9, 63-75.

De Regt, E.R. (1988), "Labor Demand and Standard Working Time in Dutch Manufacturing, 1954-1982", in R.A. Hart, ed., "Employment, Unemployment and Labor Utilization", Unwin Hyman, London.

Dolado, J.J. (1987), "Employment, Price and Inventory in Manufacturing Industry", D. Phil. Thesis, University of Oxford.

Eichenbaum, M.S. (1984), "Rational Expectations and the Smoothing Properties of Inventories of Finished Goods", Journal of Monetary Economics 14, 71-96.

Engle, R.F. (1982), "Autoregressive Conditional Heteroskedasticity with Estimates of the Variance of U.K. Inflations", Econometrica 50, 987-1008.

Engle, R.F. and C.W.J. Granger (1987), "Co-integration and Error Correction : Representation, Estimation and Testing", Econometrica 55, 251-276.

Engle, R.F. and B.S. Yoo (1987), "Forecasting and Testing in Cointegrated Systems", Journal of Econometrics 35, 143-159.

Epstein, L.G. and M.G.S. Denny (1983), "The Multivariate Flexible Accelerator Model : Its Empirical Restrictions and an Application to U.S. Manufacturing", Econometrica 51, 647-674.

Epstein, L.G. and A.J. Yatchew (1985), "The Empirical Determination of Technology and Expectations. A Simplified Procedure", Journal of Econometrics 27, 235-258.

Escribano, A. (1987), "Error-correction Systems : Nonlinear Adjustments to Linear Long-run Relationships", 29 pages.

Fuller, W.A. (1976), Introduction to Statistical Time Series, New York, Wiley.

Gallant, A.R. (1987), Nonlinear Statistical Models, New York, John Wiley.

Geweke, J.F. (1978), "Testing the Exogeneity Specification in the Complete Dynamic Simultaneous Equation Model", Journal of Econometrics 7, 163-185.

Gouriéroux, C., A. Monfort, and A. Trognon (1985), "Moindres Carrés Asymptotiques", Annales de l'INSEE 58, 91-122.

Hamermesh, D.S. (1988), "Labor Demand and the Structure of Adjustment Costs", National Bureau of Economic Research, Working Paper No. 2572.

Hannan, E.J. and L. Kavalieris (1984), "Multivariate Linear Time Series Models", Advances in Applied Probability 16, 492-561.

Hansen, L.P. (1982), "Large Sample Properties of Generalized Methods of Moments Estimators", Econometrica 50, 1029-1054.

Hansen, L.P. and T.J. Sargent (1980), "Formulating and Estimating Dynamic Linear Rational Expectations Models", Journal of Economic Dynamics and Control 2, 7-46.

Hansen, L.P. and T.J. Sargent (1981), "Formulating and Estimating Dynamic Linear Rational Expectation Models", in Rational Expectations and Econometric Practice, ed. by R.E. Lucas, Jr., and T. Sargent, Minneapolis : University Minnesota Press.

Hansen, L.P. and K. Singleton (1982), "Generalized Instrumental Variables Estimation of Nonlinear Rational Expectations Models", Econometrica 50, 1269-1286.

Harris, R.I.D. (1985), "Interrelated Demand for Factors of Production in the U.K. Engineering Industry, 1968-1981", The Economic Journal 95, 1049-1068.

Holly, S. and P. Smith (1986), "Interrelated Factor Demands for Manufacturing : A Dynamic Translog Cost Function Approach", Centre for Economic Forecasting, London Business School, discussion paper 18-86.

Holt, C.C., F. Modigliani, J.F. Muth and H.A. Simon (1960), Planning Production, Inventories and Work Force, New Jersey, Prentice-Hall.

Hosking, J.R.M. (1980), "The Multivariate Portmanteau Statistic", JASA 75, 602-608.

Kennan, J. (1979), "The Estimation of Partial Adjustment Models with Rational Expectations", Econometrica 47, 1441-1455.

Kokkelenberg, E.C. (1984), "The Specification and Estimation of Interrelated Factor Demand under Uncertainty", Journal of Economic Dynamics and Control 7, 181-207.

Kokkelenberg, E.D. and C.W. Bischoff (1986), "Expectations and Factor Demand", Review of Economics and Statistics 65, 423-431.

Kollintzas, T. (1985), "The Symmetric Linear Rational Expectations Model", Econometrica 53, 963-976.

Kydland, F. and E. Prescott (1982), "Time to Build and Aggregate Fluctuations", Econometrica 50, 1345-1371.

Liu, L.M., G.B. Hudak, G.E.P. Box, M.E. Muller, and G.C. Tiao (1986), The SCA Statistical System - Reference Manual for Forecasting and Time Series Analysis, Illinois : SCA-Press.

Ljung, G.M. and G.E.P. Box (1978), "On a Measure of Lack of Fit in Time Series Models", Biometrika 65, 297-303.

Lucas, R.E. Jr. (1976), "Econometric Policy Evaluation : A Critique", in The Phillips Curve and Labor Markets, ed. by K. Brunner and A.H. Meltzer, Amsterdam, North-Holland, 19-46.

Lütkepohl, H. (1984), "Forecasting Contemporaneously Aggregated Vector ARMA Processes", Journal of Business & Economic Statistics 2, 201-214.

Meese, R. (1980), "Dynamic Factor Demand Schedules for Labor and Capital under Rational Expectations", Journal of Econometrics 14, 141-158.

Morrison, C.J. (1986), "Structural Models of Dynamic Factors Demand with Nonstatic Expectations : An Empirical Assessment of Alternative Expectation Specifications", International Economic Review 27, 365-386.

Morrison, C.J., and E.R. Berndt (1981), "Short-run Labor Productivity in a Dynamic Model", Journal of Econometrics 16, 339-365.

McCallum, B.T. (1976), "Rational Expectations and the Natural Rate Hypothesis : Some Consistent Estimates", Econometrica 44, 43-52.

McIntosh, J. (1982), "Dynamic Interrelated Factor Demand Systems : The United Kingdom 1950-1978", The Economic Journal 92, Conference Papers Supplement, 79-86.

Nadiri, M.I. and S. Rosen (1969), "Interrelation Factor Demand Functions", American Economic Review 59, 457-471.

Nadiri, M.I. and S. Rosen (1974), A Disequilibrium Model of Demand for Factors of Production, New York, NBER.

Neftçi, S.H. (1978), "A Time Series Analysis of the Real Wages-Employment Relationship", Journal of Political Economy 86, 281-291.

Nickell, S.J. (1984), "An Investigation of the Determinants of Manufacturing Employment in the United Kingdom", Review of Economic Studies 51, 529-557.

Nickell, S.J. (1985), "Error Correction, Partial Adjustment and all that : an expository note", Oxford Bulletin of Economic and Statistics 47, 119-129.

Nickell, S.J. (1986), "Dynamic Models of Labour Demand", in O. Ashenfelter and R. Layars, eds., Handbook of Labor Economics, Elsevier, Amsterdam.

Nickell, S.J. and J. Symons (1987), "The Real Wage - Employment Relationship in the United States", Working Paper, University of Oxford.

Oi, W. (1962), "Labor as a quasi-fixed factor", Journal of Political Economy 70, 538-555.

Palm, F.C. and G.A. Pfann (1990), "Interrelated Demand Rational Expectations Models for Two Types of Labour", Oxford Bulletin of Economics and Statistics 52, 45-68.

Pfann, G.A. and B. Verspagen (1989), "The Structure of Adjustment Costs for Labour in the Dutch Manufacturing Sector", Economics Letters 29, 365-371.

Pfann, G.A. and F.C. Palm (1990), "Asymmetric Adjustment Costs in Labour Demand Models", Applied Economics Discussion Paper 87, University of Oxford.

Pfann, G.A. (1990), "Economic Crisis and the Asymmetric Multivariate Flexible Accelerator Model", Département des Sciences Economiques, Working Paper 9005, Université Catholique de Louvain.

Pindyck, R.S. and J.J. Rotemberg (1983a), "Dynamic Factor Demands and the Effects of Energy Price Shocks", American Economic Review 73, 1066-1079.

Pindyck, R.S. and J.J. Rotemberg (1983b), "Dynamic Factor Demands under Rational Expectations", Scandinavian Journal of Economics 85, 223-238.

Rossi, P.E. (1987), "Comparison of Dynamic Factor Demand Models", 357-376, in Barnett W.A., E.R. Berndt, and H. White (eds.) : Dynamic Econometric Modeling, Cambridge, Cambridge University Press.

Sargan, J.D. and A. Bhargava (1983), "Testing Residuals from Least Squares Regression for Being Generated by the Gaussian Random Walk", _Econometrica_ 51, 153-174.

Sargent, T.J. (1978), "Estimation of Dynamic Labor Demand Schedules under Rational Expectations", _Journal of Political Economy_ 86, 1009-1044.

Sargent, T.J. (1979), _Macroeconomic Theory_, New York, Academic Press.

Shapiro, M.D. (1986), "Dynamic Demand for Capital and Labor", _Quarterly Journal of Economics_ 101, 513-542.

Sims, C.A. (1980), "Macroeconomics and Reality", _Econometrica_ 48, 1-47.

Smith, D. (1984), "Short Run Employment Functions when the Speed of Adjustment Depends on the Unemployment Rate", _Review of Economics and Statistics_ 66, 138-142.

Tiao, G.C. and G.E.P. Box (1981), "Modeling Multiple Time Series with Applications", _Journal of American Statistical Association_ 76, 802-816.

Tinsley, P. (1971), "A Variable Adjustment Model of Labor Demand", _International Economic Review_ 12, 482-510.

Treadway, A.B. (1971), "The Rational Multivariate Flexible Accelerator", _Econometrica_ 39, 845-855.

Vol. 292: I. Tchijov, L. Tomaszewicz (Eds.), Input-Output Modeling. Proceedings, 1985. VI, 195 pages. 1987.

Vol. 293: D. Batten, J. Casti, B. Johansson (Eds.), Economic Evolution and Structural Adjustment. Proceedings, 1985. VI, 382 pages. 1987.

Vol. 294: J. Jahn, W. Krabs (Eds.), Recent Advances and Historical Development of Vector Optimization. VII, 405 pages. 1987.

Vol. 295: H. Meister, The Purification Problem for Constrained Games with Incomplete Information. X, 127 pages. 1987.

Vol. 296: A. Börsch-Supan, Econometric Analysis of Discrete Choice. VIII, 211 pages. 1987.

Vol. 297: V. Fedorov, H. Läuter (Eds.), Model-Oriented Data Analysis. Proceedings, 1987. VI, 239 pages. 1988.

Vol. 298: S.H. Chew, Q. Zheng, Integral Global Optimization. VII, 179 pages. 1988.

Vol. 299: K. Marti, Descent Directions and Efficient Solutions in Discretely Distributed Stochastic Programs. XIV, 178 pages. 1988.

Vol. 300: U. Derigs, Programming in Networks and Graphs. XI, 315 pages. 1988.

Vol. 301: J. Kacprzyk, M. Roubens (Eds.), Non-Conventional Preference Relations in Decision Making. VII, 155 pages. 1988.

Vol. 302: H.A. Eiselt, G. Pederzoli (Eds.), Advances in Optimization and Control. Proceedings, 1986. VIII, 372 pages. 1988.

Vol. 303: F.X. Diebold, Empirical Modeling of Exchange Rate Dynamics. VII, 143 pages. 1988.

Vol. 304: A. Kurzhanski, K. Neumann, D. Pallaschke (Eds.), Optimization, Parallel Processing and Applications. Proceedings, 1987. VI, 292 pages. 1988.

Vol. 305: G.-J.C.Th. van Schijndel, Dynamic Firm and Investor Behaviour under Progressive Personal Taxation. X, 215 pages. 1988.

Vol. 306: Ch. Klein, A Static Microeconomic Model of Pure Competition. VIII, 139 pages. 1988.

Vol. 307: T.K. Dijkstra (Ed.), On Model Uncertainty and its Statistical Implications. VII, 138 pages. 1988.

Vol. 308: J.R. Daduna, A. Wren (Eds.), Computer-Aided Transit Scheduling. VIII, 339 pages. 1988.

Vol. 309: G. Ricci, K. Velupillai (Eds.), Growth Cycles and Multisectoral Economics: the Goodwin Tradition. III, 126 pages. 1988.

Vol. 310: J. Kacprzyk, M. Fedrizzi (Eds.), Combining Fuzzy Imprecision with Probabilistic Uncertainty in Decision Making. IX, 399 pages. 1988.

Vol. 311: R. Färe, Fundamentals of Production Theory. IX, 163 pages. 1988.

Vol. 312: J. Krishnakumar, Estimation of Simultaneous Equation Models with Error Components Structure. X, 357 pages. 1988.

Vol. 313: W. Jammernegg, Sequential Binary Investment Decisions. VI, 156 pages. 1988.

Vol. 314: R. Tietz, W. Albers, R. Selten (Eds.), Bounded Rational Behavior in Experimental Games and Markets. VI, 368 pages. 1988.

Vol. 315: I. Orishimo, G.J.D. Hewings, P. Nijkamp (Eds.), Information Technology: Social and Spatial Perspectives. Proceedings, 1986. VI, 268 pages. 1988.

Vol. 316: R.L. Basmann, D.J. Slottje, K. Hayes, J.D. Johnson, D.J. Molina, The Generalized Fechner-Thurstone Direct Utility Function and Some of its Uses. VIII, 159 pages. 1988.

Vol. 317: L. Bianco, A. La Bella (Eds.), Freight Transport Planning and Logistics. Proceedings, 1987. X, 568 pages. 1988.

Vol. 318: T. Doup, Simplicial Algorithms on the Simplotope. VIII, 262 pages. 1988.

Vol. 319: D.T. Luc, Theory of Vector Optimization. VIII, 173 pages. 1989.

Vol. 320: D. van der Wijst, Financial Structure in Small Business. VII, 181 pages. 1989.

Vol. 321: M. Di Matteo, R.M. Goodwin, A. Vercelli (Eds.), Technological and Social Factors in Long Term Fluctuations. Proceedings. IX, 442 pages. 1989.

Vol. 322: T. Kollintzas (Ed.), The Rational Expectations Equilibrium Inventory Model. XI, 269 pages. 1989.

Vol. 323: M.B.M. de Koster, Capacity Oriented Analysis and Design of Production Systems. XII, 245 pages. 1989.

Vol. 324: I.M. Bomze, B.M. Pötscher, Game Theoretical Foundations of Evolutionary Stability. VI, 145 pages. 1989.

Vol. 325: P. Ferri, E. Greenberg, The Labor Market and Business Cycle Theories. X, 183 pages. 1989.

Vol. 326: Ch. Sauer, Alternative Theories of Output, Unemployment, and Inflation in Germany: 1960–1985. XIII, 206 pages. 1989.

Vol. 327: M. Tawada, Production Structure and International Trade. V, 132 pages. 1989.

Vol. 328: W. Güth, B. Kalkofen, Unique Solutions for Strategic Games. VII, 200 pages. 1989.

Vol. 329: G. Tillmann, Equity, Incentives, and Taxation. VI, 132 pages. 1989.

Vol. 330: P.M. Kort, Optimal Dynamic Investment Policies of a Value Maximizing Firm. VII, 185 pages. 1989.

Vol. 331: A. Lewandowski, A.P. Wierzbicki (Eds.), Aspiration Based Decision Support Systems. X, 400 pages. 1989.

Vol. 332: T.R. Gulledge, Jr., L.A. Litteral (Eds.), Cost Analysis Applications of Economics and Operations Research. Proceedings. VII, 422 pages. 1989.

Vol. 333: N. Dellaert, Production to Order. VII, 158 pages. 1989.

Vol. 334: H.-W. Lorenz, Nonlinear Dynamical Economics and Chaotic Motion. XI, 248 pages. 1989.

Vol. 335: A.G. Lockett, G. Islei (Eds.), Improving Decision Making in Organisations. Proceedings. IX, 606 pages. 1989.

Vol. 336: T. Puu, Nonlinear Economic Dynamics. VII, 119 pages. 1989.

Vol. 337: A. Lewandowski, I. Stanchev (Eds.), Methodology and Software for Interactive Decision Support. VIII, 309 pages. 1989.

Vol. 338: J.K. Ho, R.P. Sundarraj, DECOMP: an Implementation of Dantzig-Wolfe Decomposition for Linear Programming. VI, 206 pages. 1989.

Vol. 339: J. Terceiro Lomba, Estimation of Dynamic Econometric Models with Errors in Variables. VIII, 116 pages. 1990.

Vol. 340: T. Vasko, R. Ayres, L. Fontvieille (Eds.), Life Cycles and Long Waves. XIV, 293 pages. 1990.

Vol. 341: G.R. Uhlich, Descriptive Theories of Bargaining. IX, 165 pages. 1990.

Vol. 342: K. Okuguchi, F. Szidarovszky, The Theory of Oligopoly with Multi-Product Firms. V, 167 pages. 1990.

Vol. 343: C. Chiarella, The Elements of a Nonlinear Theory of Economic Dynamics. IX, 149 pages. 1990.

Vol. 344: K. Neumann, Stochastic Project Networks. XI, 237 pages. 1990.

Vol. 345: A. Cambini, E. Castagnoli, L. Martein, P. Mazzoleni, S. Schaible (Eds.), Generalized Convexity and Fractional Programming with Economic Applications. Proceedings, 1988. VII, 361 pages. 1990.

Vol. 346: R. von Randow (Ed.), Integer Programming and Related Areas. A Classified Bibliography 1984–1987. XIII, 514 pages. 1990.

Vol. 347: D. Ríos Insua, Sensitivity Analysis in Multi-objective Decision Making. XI, 193 pages. 1990.

Vol. 348: H. Störmer, Binary Functions and their Applications. VIII, 151 pages. 1990.

Vol. 349: G.A. Pfann, Dynamic Modelling of Stochastic Demand for Manufacturing Employment. VI, 158 pages. 1990.